The blahs! Even Christians have them! And the down time blahs can banish you to the pits. But ... there's hope ... not magic answers ... but hope ... in workable principles. Dobbert's series of sequential exercises will allow you to effectively minimize or eliminate the blahs' pitfalls and enjoy a healthy, effective attitude towards life and living. This is a great book for banishing the blahs—not you—to the pits.... Every Christian should have it!

If Being a Christian Is So Great, Why Do I Have The BLAHS?

John Dobbert

GL Regal Books A Division of G/L Publications
Glendale, California, U.S.A.

Other good Regal reading:
Do I Have to Be Me? by Lloyd H. Ahlem
Your Churning Place by Robert L. Wise
When There Is No Miracle by Robert L. Wise

The foreign language publishing of all Regal books is under the direction of GLINT. GLINT provides financial and technical help for the adaptation, translation and publishing of books in more than 85 languages for millions of people worldwide.

For more information write: GLINT, 110 W. Broadway, Glendale, California 91204.

Published by Regal Books Division, G/L Publications
Glendale, California 91209
Printed in U.S.A.

Library of Congress Catalog Card No. 79-65420
ISBN 0-8307-0729-8

In memory of Floyd Olsen,
a treasured friend and brother in Christ
who gave his life in Viet Nam

Contents

Introduction

If your life is ample and overflowing with joy, read no more. But if you can't make that claim, read on. There's hope for both of us.

You and I as Christians can live the most exciting and fulfilling life of anyone on earth. If we're not doing so, it's by our own choosing. We alone are the limiting factors. Christ Himself said, "I have come that you might have life and that you might have it more abundantly." Unless we doubt His Word or His ability to pull it off, I've got to believe His offer is still open.

Yet at times, I have the blahs so bad, I can't even relate to the victorious, abundant Christian life. Over and over I establish behavior patterns based upon my comfort and desires, paying little or no attention to Christ's blueprint for the exciting life He offers. When I choose my way rather than His I say no to growth and resume my stagnant Christian life, and the potential for excitement and joy remains untapped.

God's Word is full of verses that instruct us to grow: "Grow in the grace and knowledge of our Lord and Savior Jesus Christ. To Him be the glory, both now and to the day of eternity" (2 Pet. 3:18). "Therefore leaving the elementary teaching about the Christ, let us press on to maturity" (Heb.

6:1). "For I am confident of this very thing, that He who began a good work in you will perfect it until the day of Christ Jesus" (Phil. 1:6).

Paul urges us to grow, "so that the body of Christ may be built up until we all reach unity in the faith and in the knowledge of the Son of God and become mature, attaining to the whole measure of the fullness of Christ" (Eph. 4:12,13, *NIV*).

But few of us have found a way to translate the message contained in these verses into our daily lives. Over and over I've resolved to act on these verses yet my spiritual life remains devoid of growth. What occasional growth spurts and mountaintop experiences I do have are more than offset by extended periods of stagnancy. I respond to crisis situations by growing close to God, only to back off into my previous spiritual rut after He's seen me through.

I'm both envious and guilty when I observe persons who seem to steadily experience spiritual growth and maturity. "Don't they ever succumb to the spiritual blahs like me?"

Frequently I question, "Is it possible to live consistently on a spiritual high?" If it isn't possible, are there areas of my life that could be changed, resulting in growth and increased fulfillment?

Sure there are, and that's what this book is all about.

The candid discussion that follows lets you in on some of my habits which have greatly inhibited my spiritual growth and resulted in the "blahs" which I experience all too frequently as a child of God.

Let's examine these areas together, for you may find we share the same problems, yet feel there should be more to life. Read about these problems, you'll discover a marvelous truth: when we're open to evaluating our established practices and modifying them to correlate with His Word, excitement and joy will begin to surge into our Christian life.

I've got so far to go, but the taste of excitement I have

experienced through the strategies I describe in the pages that follow have only whet my appetite for what God has in store for those of us who love Him.

At the end of each chapter is the section "Exercise for Understanding." These questions, activities and agree-disagree exercises should help you discover for yourself where your blah areas are and what you can do about them.

Exercise for Understanding

1. Identify at least two areas of your Christian life where you need to grow.

   1. Study time
   2. Prayer
   3. Firing up bad habits

2. Think of a time in your spiritual life when you grew significantly. Describe those activities you believe contributed to your growth.

   1. Returning to Convent - accountability
   2. Teaching accountability

3. What are some excuses we use in an attempt to explain our failure to grow?
   * a. I am so busy, I don't have the time to . . . .
   b. *My bad habits are so dominering*
   c. *There is so much expected of me*
   d. *I'm not worthy*
   e.

4. In the following columns, write under each heading words or phrases that you associate with "growing" and "stagnating." Then discuss your answers with the group or individual with whom you are sharing.

GROWING	STAGNATING
a. maturing	a. boring
b. learning	b. lazy
c. new responsibility	c. decaying
d. exciting	d. dead
e. broadening	e. unattractive
f. enlightening	f. bad testimony
g. good testimony	g.

1
Short-Order Christianity

Short order conveys one message loud and clear: Quickness is more important than quality.

Our time-oriented society demands quick service since most of us just don't have enough time. We often eat, drop off undeveloped film, do our banking, watch movies, pick up groceries, pick up our developed pictures, and even attend church without ever leaving our vehicles.

We frequently read condensed versions of longer articles rather than the entire manuscript; and many of us skip the best-sellers until we can see them at our local theatre.

Every student worth his salt has learned to shortcut his study time by locating the topic sentence in each paragraph, or dwelling on the summation paragraph, without focusing on the superfluous. College-bound students are encouraged to learn shorthand or speed writing while executives streamline their use of time by using the latest sophisticated stenographic equipment.

Even home cooked meals don't receive the time and attention they used to; they are expedited through the use of microwave ovens.

The media lends credibility to the effective use of time by highlighting the day's events, for those of us who don't want to watch or read about the episodes in their entirety.

As we move from one of life's drive-ins to another, we develop a habitual pattern which we mistakenly apply to other facets of our existence. In so doing we suffer deterioration in the quality of our Christian life and our impact upon others. We attempt to expedite our contacts with troubled people with our characteristic speedy efficient manner. As a result, we may have contacts with more people yet, have often, with no positive effect upon their lives.

We greet the troubled soul with a curt, "God bless you." We visit the funeral home and console with, "We'll all see him again"; we present Christ to our neighbor by reciting the "Four Spiritual Laws" over the fence; we briefly mention a couple in our prayers who are contemplating divorce; we temporarily fill in when the regular teacher is absent; we issue the Scripture, "He will not allow you to be tempted above your ability to handle it" (see 1 Cor. 10:13), when a dear friend is passing through a period of grave temptation; and we perform many other Christian duties expeditiously.

While I don't mean to belittle these outreaches, I suggest most of them assist *us* much more than the person in need. We feel much better after extending this token gesture of Christian kindness. Now with our Christian obligation out of the way, we can get back to living without that guilty feeling.

All the examples above are demonstrations of "short-order Christianity." We "touch" and go on to our next drive-in Christian duty with great rapidity. We pride ourselves on our efficiency as though our merit was measured by the number of contacts we make.

Limited Time

We rationalize the short-order efforts by pointing to all those members of the Body who aren't doing their duty. "If they all did their duty, I could really take time to minister thoroughly. I have so much to do." It is true that most of us at times are guilty of taking on too much. We know the fruitless feeling of doing many things poorly and nothing well. Much has been written about developing the ability to say no to prevent an overextension of one's self. Trying to do too much often dilutes our efforts—making them less effective or totally ineffective.

In the case of extending our Christianity to others, I suggest it is often better to do nothing than to whet the appetite of the person in need by giving him hope of future contacts which never come.

Bob was a highly successful businessman who lived in my neighborhood. Although we knew each other only casually, our periodic conversations seemed to be warm and mutually enjoyed.

What a blow to suddenly hear that Bob's checkup revealed he had terminal cancer and, barring a miracle, would live only a few months.

I knew my Christian duty and felt compelled to visit Bob and share my faith. Several times we talked in his hospital room and he shared his concerns about his wife, Shirley, and their three children. I was always uplifted by the exuberance and confidence he expressed in the face of such horrendous odds.

In a short time Bob was transferred to a different hospital for specialized treatment to which his condition seemed to respond positively. Shortly thereafter a relapse left him reeling, and the doctors sent him home to die in the surroundings he so dearly loved.

Three home visits were all I managed during those weeks, but during one of those visits Bob assured me that he belonged to the Lord and was prepared to spend eternity with Him.

When I saw Shirley so broken at the funeral I knew she would face rough times ahead.

Almost a year has passed and I've visited Shirley only

once. Yet several of our neighbors are there on a regular basis.

Maybe my "worthwhile" activities, including eldership in the church, youth worker, committee participant, and others, will someday be evaluated by my Lord when He asks, "How was my love reflected through you to Shirley when she needed it so badly?"

Quantity versus quality may well be the question.

Limited Concern

Have you been close to someone who has lost a spouse after many years of marriage? Even when the survivor is a Christian, her keenly felt loss is often as much as she can bear as her confused mind contemplates spending the rest of her life alone. The widowed person often seems to stand up well at the funeral home as members of the Body come in droves to extend their condolences and comfort while commenting on the victorious life of the deceased and his presence in eternity. Some solace may indeed be gained through these well-intentioned statements.

The burial completed, the grieving widow returns home and the loneliness sets in. As the weeks roll by, her loneliness intensifies, as every piece of furniture and clothing remind her of her departed mate.

Five hundred people at the funeral, but now when she really needs them: "Where have all the Christians gone?" She desperately needs love, empathy, a listener, a friend, a prayermate during these lonely months which follow, yet none are to be found because we've already done our duty and have now moved along to the next in line for our dose of short-order Christianity.

Jesus Christ set a pattern which we often overlook. He ministered to many while He was on earth. Then, when He knew He would be returning to the Father, He asked the Father to send a Comforter.

Why?

The omniscient One knew that members of the human race couldn't go it alone. He knew we needed guidance, fellowship, understanding, and the peace that only He could give. Had Jesus remained on earth and lived to a ripe old age, I contend He would have developed the most intricate follow-up program that ever existed.

That follow-up program now becomes our responsibility as members of the Body of Christ.

Gourmet Christianity

Let's not "touch and go" just to satisfy our needs and lessen our guilt. Let's not give each other short-order Christianity, but concentrate on administering gourmet Christianity. Jesus gave us this treatment when He secured the services of the Comforter. This "gourmet Christianity," like a gourmet meal, has the following characteristics:

● It takes much more care and effort to prepare and serve.

● It costs more. (May require the sacrifice of our favorite pastime.)

● It involves a greater gift of our time. (Time says, "I care.")

● It is never rushed. (Although Jesus had many demands on His time, when asked a question He often related an entire parable.)

● It involves many courses. (Repeated courses are important, since they ultimately break down the barrier which often exists at first, preventing two people from really knowing each other.)

● It involves more of the real and natural and less of the artificial. (Repeated contacts allow people to know each other more deeply. This depth and trust encourage the shedding of masks we often wear.)

● It involves better quality ingredients. (When you then

observe real needs the tendency is to work harder in order to meet them.)

• It emphasizes quality, not quantity. (The fulfillment you receive is directly proportionate to your success in meeting the needs of those being ministered to.)

• It caters to one's individual taste, desires and needs. (Repeated encounters reveal these deeper needs. Knowing specific needs, you may personalize the ministry to meet them.)

Some of us hesitate to become involved in the lives of others because we are uncomfortable, feel inadequate, and "just don't know what to say." This hesitation will cease when we reach out and find that our mere presence and willingness to listen bring great blessing and comfort.

Once the person we are ministering to has experienced "gourmet Christianity" he is reminded of his importance as an individual. He savors the concern and love we extend, and the weight of his burdens seem lightened as he feels the uplifting foundational support of Jesus Christ and us. We serve in the capacity of a mirror reflecting the *agape* love of Christ.

Best of all, through our efforts and Christ's healing power, the person in need recovers to the level that he too desires to reach out to extend "gourmet Christianity" to others. Focusing on helping others is often a most important step in aiding one's own recovery.

It seems strange but as we focus on others and minister to them in a quality manner, we ourselves receive riches untold as our life takes on an added dimension of fullness. This blessing is only available through extending to others gourmet Christianity rather than the short-order kind.

Sue had been on our staff only one year before she burst into my office with tears streaming down her face. Less than six months before many on our faculty had wished her and her new husband our best wishes.

Now she sobbed as she poured her heart out. "This

marriage will never make it; he quit another job; he abuses me; he has more problems than you can imagine. I've just got to talk; can we?''

That hour we spent together became a regular happening. It kept on through her continued problems, her subsequent divorce, her loneliness, her job problems as a result of her unsettledness, and her search for a new relationship. I was there and regularly committed Sue to the Lord in prayer. Then I moved to another job location while she remained. Four years passed before I again talked with Sue at length. One day into my office walked Sue. She was beaming from ear to ear and obviously on top of the world.

She told me she had given her life to Christ and married a Christian man. They love Christ together, are active in a fellowship and want Christ to be Lord of their home.

Then she concluded: ''John, it was your willingness to see me and let me talk that got me through my problems. Because you were so kind, I felt someday I would find a man with whom I could relate. I just wanted to say thanks for sharing your faith, for being there and understanding me.''

Through tears of joy, we hugged and she left.

The Lord brought great joy into my life that day as a result of my allowing Him to work through my availability. Looking back I remembered that I had occasionally said to myself, ''Oh, no, here she comes again. I can't take time now, I've got too much to do.''

Thanks, Lord, for demonstrating the importance of being available and for reinforcing the fact that even when we feel unwilling and put-upon you see fit to bless and encourage us to practice gourmet Christianity. Help us also to be well-pleased to impart to others not only the gospel of God but also our own lives, because others are very dear to us (see 1 Thess. 2:8).

''Let us have no imitation Christian love'' (Rom. 12:9,

Phillips), *for only our Saviour's genuine love extended through us to others in need will add the dimension of joy to which you claim we're entitled.*

Exercise for Understanding

1. Is it possible to transmit gourmet Christianity without saying a word? How?

   By writing a word; a gift
   Constant prayer;

2. Read the words below and describe the thoughts that first come to mind in relation to caring for others.

   Time   *Lots*

   Guilt   *From not enough time*

   Fulfilling   *to see others happy*

   Fear   *How to approach others*

   Acceptance   *I need to accept people*
   wherever they are in life

   Love   *I show little of*

   Duty   *Commandment*

3. Think of a sorrowful experience you've been through and the person who most effectively ministered to you. What positive characteristics did they display that caused you to be open to their ministry?

   Pat Kearney because of his
   time & testimony; his devotion
   to God

2
Selective Fellowshipping

As soon as they entered the door of Calvary Community I knew we would become good friends. They appeared to be in our age bracket. She was tall, lean and tan; he well-groomed and obviously an executive. As they walked past us, Dottie and I agreed that we had to become acquainted with this new couple. When the service was completed we introduced ourselves. In subsequent months our friendship blossomed as we planned a variety of activities together. Our friendship is enriching. They now belong to our monthly gourmet group and we frequently enjoy social functions together.

Ironically, we were first attracted to Denny and Cathy because of their appearance. I must admit using this criterion as the basis for establishing a friendship is certainly suspect. But it fit in with the rest of my preconceived criteria for establishing friendships:

Avoid those younger. They make you feel like one of the Medicare set far before your time.

Avoid those older. Their maturity and solemnness will obviously eliminate any semblance of fun and will rob you of youth. At the same time, they'll always be dispensing advice based upon their vast experience.

Avoid those obviously very poor. Fellowshipping with

those in need makes it incumbent upon you to share your material blessings or experience guilt feelings for being better off.

Avoid the rich. When I'm with the rich, others may feel my association with them is based upon the hope they will add to my stature. Their ability to compile wealth also creates in me a feeling of ''what have you been doing your whole life?''

By all means avoid ministers. I can flash a Sunday smile with the best of them while congratulating the pastor for his eloquent sermon, but enough is enough. A social life involving a minister and his family would certainly be beyond the call of duty. I couldn't be myself without being continually on guard not to offend them. Besides, others might think our association was based upon our desire for status or to bolster our sagging, dilapidated spiritual condition.

All of my preconceived criteria were disproved. Shortly after our new friendship with Denny and Cathy had blossomed, we noticed the warmth of another new couple. The rapid growth of our church made it difficult to keep pace with those in our congregation each week. Only later did we discover that Karl and Sharon had been attending for several months.

Karl was a distinguished, silver haired individual. He and Sharon, his wife of English extraction, were in their fifties. We normally would have limited our contact with them to exchanging a few pleasantries in the friendly confines of the church setting. After all, they were our seniors by at least 10 years and there were several couples our own age we hadn't met yet.

Every Sunday we sought each other out and pleasantries became conversations and conversations became sharing needs and praising the Lord together. We discovered a sensitivity, empathy, openness and warmth about the Carlings that made us reach out and seek more of their fellowship.

On one hand, we sought to establish a friendship believing that Denny and Cathy were "our kind" of people. On the other hand, the Lord attracted us to Karl and Sharon even though our human nature was saying, "They're older; stay in your own age bracket."

This vivid personal illustration gave credence to the fact that our lives are often enriched by whomever the Lord sends our way. By excluding some people as a result of our preconceived ideas, we limit our blessings and theirs.

We now have dear friends with whom we regularly fellowship who are older, younger, richer or poorer and, believe it or not, in the ministry. All have deeply enriched our life. The loss of any from our fellowship would be felt greatly.

The pastor and his wife entered our lives almost two years ago. They are totally natural and seemingly devoid of pretense. We have felt accepted and loved and trust we have contributed as much to their lives as they have ours. The rewards we've received have been many.

Our lives are enriched by association with so many. The Lord in His masterful way has placed people in our lives as pieces in a puzzle, each with their own special and varied contributions.

Don contributes warmth, Sue a sweet spirit, Tom ambition, Linda optimism, Joan hospitality, Mel discipline, Hubert calmness, Bobbie vivaciousness, Jerry determination, Gloria sensitivity, Bev gentleness, Dan artistry, Marilyn patience, Dave openness, Larry dedication, Becky supportiveness, Bill enthusiasm, Nancy talent, Carol loyalty, Wayne diligence, Jim wisdom, Bob concern, Dave generosity, Larry faithfulness, Denny humor, Kathy honesty, and all love.

These and many more constitute the pieces to our puzzle of happiness which the Lord has assembled.

Lord, we anxiously await further additions to our life. We pray that we may be sensitive and receptive to all those you send our way.

Not only do we as individuals practice selective fellowship, but society and the church also seem to legislate, or at least nurture, selective fellowship.

Criteria for Selecting

For some time, the clientele of mobile home parks was almost exclusively elderly. Older folks gathered together for mutual benefits: protection, more reasonable rents, and reduced home upkeep. Some parks actually prohibited children as residents, eliminating the possibility of healthful fellowship between various age levels. However, in recent years this has been changing. I'm glad to see the present trend towards a healthful age integration of parks.

But many of our churches still practice this type of selective fellowship. As the Sunday School bell rings, millions of people leave the age integrated classes and cloister with their own age groups. The junior high, the young marrieds, the college and career group, the thirties, the forties and on up the line gather in exclusivity to guard against infiltration of the older who could share their experiences, or the younger who, seeking independence, may challenge established traditions.

While I realize the benefits that can be derived from age-level groupings, I wonder if some alternate plan might be adopted, if we truly wish to encourage true fellowship.

Romans 2:11 assures us that God does not show favoritism. Yet we, His creation, often choose those with whom we wish to associate to the exclusion of others. We, who've accepted Christ as our personal Saviour, should assume certain responsibilities, not the least of which is accepting others and extending Christ's love through us to them.

What happens when a visitor enters our church or home? Are we guilty of turning from the group we're conversing with to offer our usual canned greeting before turning our back on the newcomer and resuming our conversation? Do we really feel the, "You're-new-to-our-group-aren't-you-

welcome-to-First-Presbyterian'' is going to make the new
family feel accepted? If we do, we aren't very astute in the art
of human relations. The canned welcome we offer is as
meaningless to those who receive it as it is to us who give it.
At most it somewhat alleviates the guilt we might feel if we
had purposely avoided welcoming the visitors entirely.

Our selective fellowship isn't limited to new encounters,
however. Most fellowships are earmarked by numerous little
groups of believers who regularly gravitate together. They
always sit together in the third or fourth pew, meet for brunch
after the early service, or drive together to the Saturday
evening potluck dinner.

The criteria for forming these groups is varied but usually
incorporates several of the following:

The people involved have approximately the same—
—level of spirituality (at least in their own eyes)
—status of employment
—socio-economic strata (homes and material possessions
   fall within acceptable limits)
—educational level
—social status.

Or they are—
—members of the same country club, association or service
   club
—involved in church leadership
—alumni of the same college or group
—interested in the same hobbies
—sports fans.

Or their children—
—are in the same age bracket
—attend private schools together.

Selection Means Limitation

These are all valid reasons for establishing a fellowship
group that provides stability, security and a feeling of belong-

ing. But the harm comes when we are so selective in our fellowship that others are closed out. When this happens, the group becomes stagnant and self-centered and often inhibits the growth of an entire fellowship and later proves to be a source of divisiveness.

Most human beings are creatures of comfort. We come in from the cold, eat when hunger pains ensue, and automatically withdraw from threatening situations. For many of us, meeting new people and establishing new relationships incorporate elements of risk and discomfort. We find it easier to withdraw to the safety and security of our tried and proven friendships, those who accept us as they see us. But we are afraid to venture into the unknown where new acquaintances may exercise their option to reject us.

Not only are we afraid of rejection, we are also afraid of acceptance. A natural outgrowth of a new friendship is its development into love. And we're well aware that when we open up to love, we're more susceptible to hurt and ''the Lord knows we've been hurt enough.'' Why risk more loving relationships which may increase our chances of being devastated?

We don't expand our fellowship, many times, because we ''don't have time.'' The greatest fulfillments in life often come via personal relationships, thus we seek to establish quality ones. We weed out those we feel we wouldn't hit it off with and attempt to nourish those who attract us. Nurturing these desired friendships requires the expenditure of time and effort, so a goodly number rationalize, ''I can only have a few close friendships. My time doesn't allow for more.''

Absurd as it seems, some members of the Body take a passive role towards newcomers on the belief that their capacity to extend love is limited. When God is put to the test, He disproves this theory since He's devoid of limitations. We, as believers, have access to an unlimited supply of His love to extend to all comers. We alone, unwilling to draw from His infinite love supply, inject the only limiting factor.

When newcomers believe themselves to be precluded from the inner circle of fellowship, they evaluate the entire Body as unfriendly and hypocritical. If they feel unaccepted they will soon be absent from this fellowship. If their experience leads them to believe that all Christians talk about unconditional love yet few, if any, practice what they preach, the cliquish Christians may, through their hypocriticalness, be responsible for arresting spiritual growth or contributing to the hardness of the hearts of those newcomers who originally came seeking fellowship.

When numerous cliques develop within a fellowship, they automatically limit the numerical growth of the Body. Cliques prevent new people from receiving the degree of personalization necessary for them to feel important and part of the group.

Some churches have attempted to organize *koinonia* groups or congregational groups to provide the degree of personalization that is needed. At times even these configurations designed to alleviate the problem include an element of cliquishness.

Looking at fellowships through God's eyes may necessitate us reevaluating this mode of operation. If we study the example of Jesus Christ, we see Him reaching out to all people. Looking further, we note that He never turned His back or failed to nurture any who were in need.

By selectively weeding prospective friends out, we eliminate two distinct possibilities.

First, we cannot contribute in any way to the lives of those we eliminate from our realm of contact. The gifts for ministry which God has bestowed upon us are wasted as far as those people we have excluded are concerned.

Second, those we've excluded cannot contribute to our lives. I've established many a friendship while believing I would contribute much to the life of the new friend only to find out that I received much more than I contributed. When we open ourselves to wider fellowship those we may have thought would be unlikely friends may turn out to possess qualities which allow them to make unique and wonderful contributions to our lives.

Holier Than Thou

Many who are born again feel that in reality they operate at a higher level and are better than those who've never made a commitment asking Christ into their lives.

Nothing is more obvious to a non-Christian than a Christian's attitude of superiority. Not only does it offend him but it almost always precludes any possibility of our sharing our life or our faith. An attitude of superiority prohibits communication.

Essential to sharing Christ is that others see your life horizontally. Unless they see you on the same level interest as they are they will not hear much of what you have to say.

Some believers feel they can be unfriendly and aloof most of the time yet will occasionally attempt to be spiritually lower in order to minister to those they choose not to associate with socially. What a shock they're in for as those to whom they're attempting to minister turn them off.

Sometimes Christians assume a facade that says, "I am holier than thou" in an attempt to elevate their own status. "I don't possess any detrimental habits, don't anger, am patient, kind, loving, and very spiritual."

When we do this, two things may occur, neither of which is good. First, some we're attempting to minister to may believe our facade. If they do, we appear unapproachable to them due to our "perfection." Second, others see us as phony and hypocritical. This being the case, our credibility is severely lessened and our future attempts to witness are nullified. In either case, our ministry is voided.

Some believers adopt an isolationist policy while contending that they are certainly not going to associate with those who use crude language, or smoke or who've committed crimes, are below their station in life, or who're ethnically different.

Yet Jesus Christ mixed with everyone, from Pharisee to prostitute. He spread His message, not theirs.

If we are Christians, our very life should be pulsating with the life of Christ. If it is, we will accept both believers and nonbelievers alike while proclaiming His truths.

Advantages of Unlimited Fellowship

It is true that we can't spend the same amount of time with all people, nor develop the same intense relationships with everyone. We must, however, ask the question, "Would God have sent these people into our fellowship without expecting me and others to reach out and extend love to them?"

If we're practicing selective fellowship, we must examine our motivation for doing so. Are we following this pattern because we feel better with certain people? While comfortableness is important, if it dictates our decisions, growth may be severely limited.

Do we select those who meet our own needs? We must honestly determine whether they are receiving as much fulfillment from us as we are from them. A good relationship should be mutually fulfilling.

As a church, do we seek to recruit those in prominent public positions as though God coveted their souls more than those who are lesser known? God chastised those who catered to the rich, and indicated that all of heaven rejoices when one soul comes to Him.

Others limit their contact so they may become more intimately involved with a close circle of friends. While this at times provides a therapeutic effect and great blessing, too great a degree of intimacy may later bring embarrassment and promote problems.

Selective fellowship can be as destructive to the Body of Christ as inbreeding is to subsequent generations. Let's broaden our contacts by reaching out to all we encounter and then let God determine their response to us.

Fellowship is viewed by many Christians as a "do your own thing" enterprise. As I read the Scriptures, however, I read that it should really be "do God's thing." He created us for the purpose of fellowshipping with Him and also fellow-shipping with others. If we, by our own design, limit our contacts, we may be limiting our potential to be used by the Holy Spirit. When our potential is limited, our blessing is limited, and life lacks the fulfillment which could be ours.

"He who ministers to one of mine, really does so to me" (see Matt. 25:40). These words of Jesus tell us that when we minister (and ministering is an outgrowth of fellowship) to others, we are actually ministering to our Saviour. Does that put open fellowship in the proper perspective?

We praise God by accepting others. "Accept one another, just as Christ also accepted us to the glory of God" (Rom. 15:7). Can you imagine that we, by truly accepting those who come into our lives, are used as a vehicle to bring praise to God?

Fellowshipping with others brings us rich blessings. "There is one who scatters, yet increases all the more, and there is one who withholds what is justly due, but it results only in want" (Prov. 11:24). When we give of ourselves freely to others while accepting them in love, the Lord richly blesses us in accordance with His promise.

My life, and I'm sure yours, is enriched regularly by contributions through fellowship with old friends, new acquaintances, and persons God allows to come into our path.

Let's strive to reach out and share our lives with them and claim His promise that their lives will be enriched, our lives will be blessed, and our Saviour will be praised.

To do anything less by selectively limiting those with

whom we choose to fellowship, severely lessens our potential fulfillment as well as that of those God has placed in our lives.

Lord, today make me aware that you bring people into my life for a purpose. Help me show your warmth, love and acceptance to all. May your Holy Spirit make me sensitive to their needs as you are to mine. Thanks for all those you've placed in my life.

Exercise for Understanding

1. List actions (subtle or overt) that you may take (consciously or unconsciously) which may give a newcomer a feeling of inclusion or exclusion.

   Inclusion   Exclusion
   a.
   b.
   c.
   d.
   e.
   f.

2. Reflect upon your closest friends and list their names below. Next to each name list the quality which attracted you to that person, allowing friendship to blossom:
   a.

   b.

   c.

3. Should you consider breaking up an established Bible study group (meeting two years) which seems to meet a vital need for all participants in order to spread the leadership potential and involve new people?

4. How does the following verse have application to fellowship? "Do not merely look out for your own personal
   interests, but also for the interests of others. Have this
   attitude in yourselves which was also in Christ Jesus"
   (Phil. 2:4,5).

3
Inadequate Rejoicing

During the formative years of my Christian life I was taught the vital skill of bearing others' burdens and sharing their sorrows. Only recently did I discover that all that bearing and sharing could lead to the blahs unless it was counterbalanced by an equal or greater amount of rejoicing.

If you're like most people who claim the name of Christ, you experience no problem feeling empathy for and showing kindness to those whom you believe to be suffering.

Our hearts, and hopefully our hands, reach out to help bear the burdens of the woman whose body is racked by cancer, the young couple whose child succumbed to sudden illness, the middle-aged woman whose husband was unfaithful, or the man who in the prime of life was unexpectedly released from the company after being with them for 20 years.

Even when we don't move in a visible way to help those who hurt, our thoughts frequently turn to them and we respond by committing their situation to Christ in prayer.

Rejoice with the Rejoicing

When we reach out to the suffering we experience a relief of sorts in knowing we have fulfilled our Christian obligation to "weep with those who weep"; yet many of us will enter the state of shock when our Master Teacher asks, "What about the other 50 percent of my command? You receive an A in *weeping;* however in *rejoicing* you get an F. Through Paul I instructed you 'Rejoice with those who rejoice, and weep with those who weep' (Rom. 12:15). Why have you neglected to do this? I deem one as important as the other."

Being convicted of negligence in this area, I wondered how I'd answer the charge.

It's so easy to empathize with the person whom we view as being worse off than ourselves. When we're well and they're sick, when our marriage is good and theirs is failing, when we're gainfully employed and they're struggling on welfare or disability, when our family appears vigorous yet one of their beloved has recently passed away, our hearts ache for them.

When, however, we are hurting or our lives are stagnantly embedded in the status quo, while everything good seems to be happening to them, does our Saviour find us rejoicing?

I submit the answer is *no,* or *rarely.*

As long as we can look down while witnessing His blessings we smile and somewhat disassociatedly say, "How nice."

Yet as God unleashes a cloudburst of blessings on our friends in the form of business or financial windfall, increased material possessions, physical health, success of the offspring, professional advancement, or harmonious relationships to the point where we view his status as now elevated above ours, an attitudinal change often occurs.

Either verbally or within the confines of our mind we question the fairness of this new development and may even claim "foul." We find it difficult to rejoice with people who appear to be doing well, for often we perceive their success as attesting to our inadequacy.

Bill and I had an excellent relationship and our families often planned outings together. We earned approximately the same salary in our respective occupations so both were accustomed to keeping a close eye on our vacation expenditures while traveling the "Holiday Inn" route.

Then Bill was given an outstanding promotion which more than doubled his salary. When he shared the way the Lord had blessed him, I outwardly told him how happy I was yet inwardly was seized by jealousy. Envy and resentment adversely affected our relationship as I observed his newly acquired financial freedom.

Then one day the Lord confronted me with the bare truth. My inability to truly rejoice with Bill was ruining my relationship with him and the Lord. I confessed my resentment to the Lord and He assured me that my worth wasn't contingent upon my annual salary. He also instructed me through His Word to rejoice with Bill.

What a relief! Joy entered my life again and soon our relationship was stronger than ever before.

Learning to Rejoice

As the person being showered with blessings is perceived by us to be forging ahead of our status, our unregenerate human nature transforms our attitude from one of empathy to one of jealousy. We rationalize his success in a variety of ways as we judgmentally ask or state (usually to another envying person):

"I wonder if he made all the money honestly?"

"It's easy to be successful when your family has money."

"His kids were just in the right place at the right time."

"Their relationship only seems good; I bet in private they're always at each other's throats."

These remarks, directed at minimizing others or putting down the blessings they have received, usually stem from our own feelings of insecurity. The secure person finds it easier to rejoice with the fortunate, for he knows that healthy feelings about himself are not dependent upon favorable comparisons with others. He feels good about himself whether viewing those who have the world by the tail or those who are experiencing critical needs.

Certainly God must have provided some assistance which will allow me to learn to be a rejoicer. "Old things passed away; behold, new things have come" (2 Cor. 5:17), says that I, through Christ, don't need to accept my natural jealous and insecure tendencies any longer. I can rejoice with others and rejoicing can be the norm for me.

"I can do all things through Him who strengthens me" (Phil. 4:13) informs me that I needn't succumb to my present tendencies unless I want to. I can be a rejoicer by appropriating His strength and applying His sufficiency to correct deficiencies in my life.

When I fail to rejoice with others, several things take place:

I am violating a command of God, and therefore displeasing Him. Either the entire command, "Rejoice with those who rejoice, and weep with those who weep" is valid and therefore applicable to our lives or all of Scripture lacks credibility. My failure to rejoice is not blessing God and may well be grieving Him.

I am robbing others of fully enjoying God's blessings. When one is the recipient of God's goodness he should be able to savor it while praising and thanking God. Nothing puts a damper on this possibility quicker than the obvious jealousy on the part of persons considered friends. The drifting apart of relationships and associated heartaches dilutes the blessings one could experience.

I am punishing myself and limiting my fulfillment. The negative emotions that permeate our being when we resent another person affect only ourselves. The person who is rejoicing is seldom aware of our feeling towards him. We pay the heavy price and often feel guilty about the unjustified feelings we're harboring.

As we spend our precious energies focusing on another's situation, we reduce the available energies to achieve other worthwhile fulfilling pursuits. This mode of operation is self-defeating.

I am lessening the power in my life. "If you abide in Me, and My words abide in you, ask whatever you wish, and it shall be done for you" (John 15:7). We abide in Christ when we are obedient to Him and His Word. When we are obedient, and that includes rejoicing, He promises us a blank check if we only ask. Failure to rejoice stamps "nonnegotiable" on the face of that check and renders us without a much needed power supply.

I am robbing myself of joy. Philippians 2:4 encourages us "do not merely look out for your own personal interests, but also for the interests of others." In verses 17 and 18 Paul states, "I rejoice and share my joy with you all. And you too, I urge you, rejoice in the same way and share your joy with me."

When we cannot share joy with our brothers and sisters in Christ (or the unsaved), we turn our back on a provision established by Christ for bringing joy into our own lives. Joy when shared is infectious and favorably influences all we endeavor to accomplish and all with whom we have contact.

I am subconsciously charging God with favoritism. Although the Scriptures declare that "there is no partiality with God" (Rom. 2:11), we frequently question in the confines of our heart, "Why did you bless him so much more than me, Lord?"

You may say "Not me," but before you utter that denial, check to see that *your attitude is not showing*. The mere fact you're not able to rejoice with others may be a tipoff that you're questioning God's "partiality."

A few years ago, I felt led of the Lord to attempt to write. Four months and hundreds of hours later, I submitted the completed manuscript and much to my surprise the Lord provided a publisher.

I could hardly wait to share my blessings with my friends. Excitedly I shared with one couple only to discover they were anything but thrilled at my news. To this day, I avoid all mention of publishing in their presence. Evidently they had not mastered the art of rejoicing. Their inability to handle my good news caused me to question, ''If the shoe were on the other foot, how would I respond?''

How healthy and joyous it would be if we as members of the Body of Christ could feel free to share with one another the victories and blessings the Lord has granted us without fear of rejection, resentment, or jealousies creeping in to diminish our relationship.

Freed Up to Share

Because of our hesitancy to share the blessings the Lord has given us and our reluctance to rejoice with others whom the Lord has blessed, Christianity has become for many a negatively oriented commodity instead of the positive daily experience Christ intended it to be. Unfortunately the Christian's creed seems to be: ''It is appropriate to share our hurts, burdens, sorrows, and needs, but by all means, avoid sharing the victories and blessings you've experienced. For your brothers and sisters in the Lord are likely to construe your declarations as bragging which would certainly affect any relationship in a negative manner.'' With this attitude prevalent in so many believers, a victorious rejoicing fellowship is nigh unto impossible since few are freed up to the extent that they'll share and risk these consequences.

Certainly there are appropriate times to share abundant blessings and times when withholding to a more appropriate time may be better. When a person conveys his deep sorrow and grief to you, it would be totally inappropriate to rejoice about your current blessings. You should be sharing his sorrow and rendering assistance to him during this time of critical need. The sharing of your blessings should come later when he's emotionally recovered, or you risk the chance of driving him to deeper depths.

Let's strive to make our faith a positive venture by accepting those who have been blessed by God and then taking that step beyond to rejoice with them. If we all made a prayerful effort to incorporate this change into our lives, a positive surge would infuse the Body of Christ, the *blessed* and the *rejoicer* would reap greater fulfillment and, best of all, our Lord would be praised.

Maybe we haven't nurtured the ability to rejoice with others because we've never asked for it. Until now you may have thought that rejoicing was unimportant, so why would you ask for it. James said, "You do not have because you do not ask" (4:2). Let's ask our Lord to give us the desire and ability to share our blessings with others while accepting others' blessings in a true spirit of rejoicing.

Paul knew the importance of rejoicing when he wrote to the church at Corinth, "And if one member suffers, all the members suffer with it; if one member is honored, all the members rejoice with it" (1 Cor. 12:26).

Let's rejoice, for rejoicing with others brings joy into our life.

Lord, it's good to know that I'm expected to rejoice with others. Free me from petty jealousies which tempt me to explain away others' blessings. Help me to share the good things you're doing in my life in a manner which would be encouraging to others.

From this day forward, allow me the healthy balance of weeping and rejoicing which I now see is so vital to a joyful life in you.

Exercise for Understanding

1. Examine your past month:
   a. Recall the times you actually rejoiced with others who were richly blessed.

   b. What decided effort will you make to increase the times of rejoicing with others this next month?

2. Describe how you feel when you harbor negative feelings towards another person.

   Realize that you are the loser physically, mentally, emotionally, psychologically and spiritually when you resent rather than rejoice.

3. Describe a time when you experienced a blessing only to have a friend respond adversely upon hearing of it.

4. Try at least one of the following activities in the near future:
   a. Write a minimum of one note per week letting someone know you're rejoicing with them.
   b. Share a personal blessing with a valued friend and encourage him to do the same with you. Nurture your ability to do this in such a way that God receives the glory.

4
Illicit Affairs

When "affair" is mentioned one usually visualizes a married man telling his wife he must remain at the office while in reality he meets his lover for a romantic interlude culminating in sexual gratification.

Or, the "loyal" married woman arranging a rendezvous with her secret lover while outwardly parading the image of love and devotion to her husband and children.

When we're cognizant of this unfaithfulness in the lives of others, we inwardly question, "How could he do that to his family?" "How could she risk everything for such a fleeting moment?"

We ask these questions with a certain amount of righteous indignation as though the same situation could never befall us who are so committed.

After all, we reason, an affair:
- Breaks the trust you've shared with your spouse since the moment you said "I do."
- Divides your affections between those you're committed to and the new recipient of your time and attentions.
- Causes you to forsake your priorities and compromise your convictions.

- Steals time which rightfully should be devoted to those for whom you're responsible.
- Produces guilt, affecting your objectivity and self-concept, therefore lessening your effectiveness as a person.
- Sets a negative example for your kids and those with whom you associate.
- Increases the chances of strife within the home.
- Brings reproach to the Body of Christ.
- Reduces your ministry to zero.
- Negatively affects your relationship with your Saviour.
- Frequently produces some deterioration of mental and physical health.

An affair is often short-lived, yet the hurt and the results which follow may leave lifetime scars. The loss of a family, the missed thrills of seeing your daughter graduate, those family gatherings you used to have on the holidays, and your boy's first touchdown pass somehow are not as exciting and significant as when you lived in the home and shared in the preparation and anticipated excitement.

Who can console and comfort that daughter more effectively than Dad when she's jilted by her first boyfriend and her world seems torn asunder?

Oh, how they've blown it. I hurt for them, don't you? So much hurt here on earth you'd think that was sufficient. God has also stated that He will judge adulterers.

The Other Affairs

Yet wait a minute. Me an affair? Not on your life. I haven't ever violated our marriage vows.

But what about "affairs" that do not involve extramarital relationships? Yes, Lord, I am guilty.

I'm having an affair with YOUR church. I meant well, honest I did. But I couldn't say no to Wednesday night, or choir practice, or teaching Sunday School, or the missionary committee. Then once I started I couldn't quit. You don't want a quitter do you, Lord? I forced my kids to attend no matter what other pressures they were facing. Even if it meant failing a school exam, they were at every meeting. After all, I am their spiritual leader. My job effectiveness even lessened, but I did it for you Lord.

Then my family started falling apart as I forsook their needs in favor of your church. I really thought it was what you'd have me to do. I put them on the altar for you Lord. I thought you'd guide them and care for them since I'm so involved for you.

Now I'm so guilty and worried about the status of my family, I can't even worship. Help me, Lord, help me.

I'm having an affair with my job. My day begins at 5:30 A.M. I get to the office at 6:30 A.M. although I'm not required to be there until 8:00. I do so to plan my day so it will be highly effective and allow me to accomplish the maximum amount of work. I am so busy in this demanding job that I work through lunch every day or eat on the run. My work day is supposed to end at 5:00 P.M., but often I stay later to tie up loose ends.

When I come home I wish I could relax with the kids and my wife, but time is money, so most nights are spent figuring out bids for my next jobs. I actually work about 18 hours a day, but I don't mind it. They'll soon see how valuable I am and move me right up the company ladder.

I'm having an affair with myself. I am important and know I am. The mere fact Someone would give His life for me verifies this fact.

I am intelligent and likable as well. I've worked hard at developing a pleasing personality. People really enjoy being around me. I have leadership qualities too. All my life people have followed me.

I rarely enter a conversation which I don't manipulate to the point where I can tell others about my outstanding qualities and positive attributes. Shouldn't we be proud of our strong points? I've been told that everyone needs a healthy self-concept.

Occasionally people express the opinion that I am conceited, but I say, "If you've got it, be proud of it." I think they're just jealous because they view themselves as inferior. I've been told that false humility is bad, so I'd just as soon take my chances of being too proud than falsely humble.

I believe I can set my goals and accomplish just about anything I want to. I am really happy and excited about my future and just can't wait to see how far I want to go.

I'm having an affair with my hobby. I love to collect stamps. Every spare moment I have finds me behind the closed door in my study involved with my collection.

It gets on my wife's nerves when I put off house maintenance chores or other tasks she deems important. But I really feel I need this hobby. I feel guilty when the kids want me to play with them, or help them with their homework, but I justify it by thinking I'll live longer if I relax through my hobby and then later I'll have more time to spend with them.

I can hardly wait to come home from work and retreat to my study. Occasionally I even play "sick" and spend all day arranging displays, planning buys, laying out ads, or calling about finances to buy collections which are on sale. In the future I hope to build this hobby into a financial success.

I do feel physically taxed at work occasionally. When you work until after midnight three or five days a week on your hobby it is a little tiring. But it sure is fun.

I just hope I can pay back all the loans I secured to buy these new collections. If I can't, I've really got some explaining to do.

I'm having an affair with food. If I'm honest, the greatest pleasure I derive in life is sitting down to a sumptuous gourmet dinner and eating until I can't eat any more. There must be better things in life, but if there are, I haven't found them yet.

At times I feel guilty about the amount I consume, but there are a lot worse things aren't there? I don't drink or smoke and I'm not immoral so I figure one indiscretion won't hurt.

As soon as I wake in the morning my thoughts are on those bacon and eggs. At coffee break time I already know what I'll have for lunch. Shortly after lunch I actually picture my dinner and long for its soothing effect. When my mate and I plan a night out at a fine restaurant I actually count the days until that evening comes, and long before the actual event I already know what I'm going to order.

Yet I seem to get everything done which is expected of me, so I guess it's all right. My love of food doesn't seem to render me inoperable, although my present physical condition does limit my rapidity of movement.

I'm having an affair with sex. It may be my age, but my sexual drive seems to be ever increasing. From the moment of fulfillment I begin thinking about the next experience.

I dwell on sex so much I actually must admit it sometimes interferes with my work. In the middle of my work-related problems I have to snap myself back from a fantasy to the world of reality.

I'm even bothered in church. If I see an attractive woman in church my mind sometimes wanders from the message and—talk about guilt! Right there in church sex comes to mind when I should be focusing on God.

I have difficulty whenever I see a beautiful woman. But that's not wrong, is it? God made those beautiful creatures, and it's a compliment to His handiwork that I enjoy studying them so much. After all, I only look. Just because you've already ordered your meal doesn't mean you can't look at the menu anymore, does it?

Clean Up Your Act

After close examination of my own affairs, I now am

aware that by pointing my finger accusingly at others, I've been guilty of violating God's Word which states "How can you say to your brother, 'Let me take the speck out of your eye,' and behold, the log is in your own eye? You hypocrite, first take the log out of your own eye; and then you will see clearly enough to take the speck out of your brother's eye" (Matt. 7:4,5). In everyday language, I know God is telling me to clean up my own act before I look at my brother's problems.

In reality, there are very few people who aren't having affairs. *Your* mistress, while posing no problem for another, is tearing your world asunder. A particular source of unfaithfulness for another offers no temptation to you. And so it goes.

The preceding situations I've described wouldn't be classified as affairs by most. In fact, most would declare them harmless when compared with the universally accepted definition of affair as "sex outside of marriage."

I submit these situations as described, plus the one you've personalized are every bit as destructive as extramarital affairs. In fact, in many cases they're more destructive since extramarital affairs are often of brief duration while the affairs described herein subtly continue to cause havoc for a lengthy duration since they do not carry the strong stigma of social or spiritual unacceptability.

Long after the extramarital affair is over and the couple have resolved their problem or established a new relationship, these other more subtle affairs continue to fester and cause deterioration in relationships with God, family, others, and self.

There is no question that sexual unfaithfulness in marriage is wrong. We know it is. The Bible declares it so, society deems it so, and even with the recent trend towards permissiveness, self-guilt of the participants sufficiently prove that a violation of morals has occurred.

Yet somehow we defend those other affairs with seemingly justifiable questions:

Shouldn't I serve the Lord?

Shouldn't I work hard and try to get ahead in my job? God's Word says, "Do all unto the glory of God" and that to me means work diligently.

Isn't it important to feel good about oneself?

Surely, a hobby is healthy, isn't it?

If food is my only vice, that's okay, isn't it?

Didn't God plan sex for our enjoyment?

All these questions can be answered affirmatively with a yes.

Then, what's wrong?

"Wrongness" enters the picture as a matter of degree. While each of these desires and activities are healthy and normal, and some downright admirable, when they begin consuming an inordinate amount of our time and effort to the degree that our priorities must be disbanded, they then assume the cloak of destructiveness.

Prioritize Your Life

Each member of the Body of Christ should assume his priorities according to the Scriptures. These priorities include:

His love for God and devotion to Him

His love for mate and devotion to spouse and family

His love for fellow Christians and devotion to them

His love for the unbelievers

His quality job performance attesting to the positive influence of his faith.

These priorities are intricately balanced and total devotion to any one level to the exclusion of the others brings disharmony on all levels and displeasure to the person who himself is the focus of that priority.

As an example, God has created us to glorify Him and one

way we do so is by serving Him. Yet if we serve Him to such an extent that we neglect duties to our family as outlined in the Scripture, He is grieved, not glorified.

The reciprocal also presents great problems. If our whole life and all our time and energies are devoted to our personal family and their needs to the exclusion of Christ's work, God is miserable, we are convicted and miserable, and even our family will reflect our miserableness.

Many mistakenly believe that God's Word encourages the reader to plunge headlong and totally into God's work while forsaking all other priorities. That couldn't be farther from the truth.

While God calls us to His service, He gives specific guidelines concerning our family, mate, children, job performance, eating, sex, hobbies, and any other subject with which you may have filled in the blank. He has taken great pains to carefully delineate our obligations in these areas so we may maintain His delicate balance which insures fulfillment.

Jesus Christ took a mortal body so that He could experience our temptations and feelings and know how to extend mercy and forgiveness to us when we stumble into an affair.

Let's not point the finger at the person who cheated on his spouse, or attempt to justify our "affair" by pointing to someone who we think has done worse. Let's extend mercy and love towards one another and, while doing so, let's examine carefully our own life and ask His forgiveness for our "affairs" and seek to remedy the situation by following His teachings regarding our priorities.

God is greater than any problem we have. He has given us complete freedom. Paul says: "It was for freedom that Christ set us free; therefore keep standing firm and do not be subject again to a yoke of slavery" (Gal. 5:1). This means that we have the option to be and remain free. To be enslaved to any external or internal influence, limits God's benefit to us (see

Gal. 5:2). Jesus (the Truth), promised, "You shall know the truth, and the truth shall make you free" (John 8:32).

If you abide in Christ and are obedient to His Word and to the leading of the Holy Spirit, then you can "ask whatever you wish [and that includes deliverance from slavery to anything in your life], and it shall be done for you" (John 15:7).

Thank you, Father, for giving me the potential to be free. If I exercise that option, Lord, I needn't any longer be enslaved to my job, my material possessions, my church, my family, my thought life, my desires, or any other controlling factor.

Thank you for showing me that enslavement to anything, even socially acceptable activities, robs me of the joy that can be mine when I live according to your priorities.

Exercise for Understanding

1. List masters (other than those included in the chapter) to whom you could be enslaved.

2. Examine Galatians 4:9. What does this verse of Scripture say to you?

3. Do you agree or disagree with the following statements?

                                                            agree   disagree

    a. It is easier to find fault in others than it is to find shortcomings in myself. ☐ ☐

    b. The shortcomings I perceive in others are frequently present in my life as well. ☐ ☐

	agree	disagree
c. Some affairs (as described within this chapter) are, in themselves, positive pursuits.	☐	☐
d. At times, God doesn't mind us forsaking our family responsibilities to benefit His work.	☐	☐
e. Guilt which comes when the Holy Spirit tells us we are violating our rightful priorities lessons our productivity.	☐	☐
f. Liberty and freedom come through enslavement to Christ.	☐	☐
g. Freedom is not the power to do what I want but the power to live the life I know I should.	☐	☐

4. As a parent, what possible impact does your having an affair have upon your children?

5
Limited Commitment

Bert had accepted the Lord as his personal Saviour during his teen years, but currently was living anything but a victorious Christian life.

While he was in college, Bert drifted away from the Lord, doing his own thing. After graduation he was the life of the party and his colleagues on the job frequently gathered around him to hear the latest off-color jokes. In later years, Bert's wife, Barbara, and three children were immersed in community functions to the point where church attendance was limited to Christmas and Easter.

A friend of Bert's was enthusiastic about a new group of believers with whom he was fellowshipping. He frequently invited Bert and his family to attend but excuses flowed freely. However, one Sunday, Bert and his family appeared in church and the Lord touched his heart.

Within a matter of months, Barbara and the three children invited Christ into their lives and the family grew together in the Lord.

Recently Bert approached the friend who united him to church. "John, the Lord has been dealing with me and has revealed that I must turn all areas of my life over to Him. Last night I vowed to refrain from telling or listening to any off-color jokes so I can be a more effective witness. Pray for me, John; that's going to be very difficult for me since I like to be the center of attraction and get the laughs.''

The Lord has given Bert victory over this area of his life and through the victory increasing joy and fulfillment.

Bert has become sensitive to the Holy Spirit and desires to bring his whole life in accord with the will of God.

How difficult it will be to stand before our Saviour and explain, with any credible rationale, why we chose to involve Him in certain areas of our lives while purposely excluding Him from others. Well, maybe a God of grace won't hold us accountable. We did say, "We turn our lives over to you, Lord," but we've got to believe He certainly realizes it's difficult to yield every area to Him.

I, for one, am really irritated at those bumper-sticker Christians who display that guilt-producing slogan, "If He isn't Lord of all, He's not Lord at all." Many professing Christians, including myself, experience great difficulty in infusing Christ into every area of our lives. We feel great fulfillment when we abundantly give to the work of the Lord, only to have the bubble pop as we float to the solid earth with the realization that an examination of our thought life would belie our declaration of Christianity.

We commit our talents to Him and glowingly sing His praises when granted the opportunity, but our obese and sloppy appearance denotes anything but sufficiency of the power of God to assist us in the area of self-control.

With principles from the Word of God, we counsel others who are experiencing marital trouble only to return home to psychologically abuse our mate.

A certain amount of pride is evident as we exhibit our straight A report card attesting to our well-developed self-discipline, yet sadness enters the picture as we must admit we haven't read the Word of God in months.

Aware of Charlie's extramarital affair, we righteously declare, "Lord, I've remained pure since my vows," then turn to stare at that shapely new employee with lust in our heart.

Content with the belief we've never purposefully told a lie with the intent of doing any harm, we proceed to pass on a rumor which murders another's reputation within the Body of believers.

We feel good that we are accepted by others as church leaders, yet experience great remorse when we must assume a degree of responsibility for our oldest child's heavy involvement in drugs.

Joy enters our life as we fellowship with other believers, yet sorrow is ours as we realize we've rarely, if ever, been responsible for introducing a friend to our King.

The Christian life seems to be filled with these dichotomies. Yet Christ certainly did not intend to introduce conflict into our lives. His Word, applied to our life, adds unity. "Yes, every area of our lives is to be under the Lordship of Jesus Christ. And that means the searchlight of God's Word must penetrate every corner of our lives. We are not free to pick and choose the parts of the Bible we want to believe or obey. God has given us all of it, and we should be obedient to all of it."[1]

Objective of Wholeness

The presence of Christ in our life should be the unifying force. Divisiveness and conflict are not of Him. We must realize that our unwillingness to submit *all areas* of our lives to Him is what causes the seeming dichotomies. If He is consistently involved in the totality of our lives, His presence will add the dimension of stability and fulfillment.

Since Christ's objective is to make us whole in every area of our lives, why then as Christians do we relegate Him to the role of a partial God by inviting Him into selected areas of our lives while declaring Him an intruder in others.

Pay-back principle. Many of us invoke the pay-back principle and bring ourselves to the point of believing that God will deal leniently with us in areas of noncompliance because we've earned it through conformity to His desires in other areas.

We try to buy God off by saying, "Lord, I've committed my talents to you, raised my family in a godly way, and I regularly support your work, surely you'll excuse me for my present cellular accumulation in excess of 300 pounds."

In case your plan for God's leniency isn't adopted, you've conspired to enter the heavenly portals between the two elephants that boarded the ark in hope you'll be accepted as normal and not viewed as a mutant.

I shudder to think about the number of times I've attempted to buy off my God by pointing to limited proficiencies and victories or by promising a more complete future commitment. How ludicrous to promise my omniscient Saviour my future compliance when He already knows the future (including whether or not I fulfilled my promises).

As Christians most of us are aware that continued noncompliance of God's principles is misuse of God's grace. We criticize the world when they adopt the policy, "If it feels good, do it," and openly declare that one's pleasure as the prime criterion for our course of action is wrong. We then continue excluding God from areas of our life in which, for a variety of reasons (often our pleasure), we want to do our own thing. If our criticism is just, certainly it's applicable to both situations. So who's calling the kettle black?

False victory—victory by default. Some righteously declare victory in areas of their lives and fully expect the plaudits of men and elevation by Christ.

At times the victory is worthy. Our brothers rejoice with the victories, and great joy undoubtedly abounds in heaven. For our growth and victories are pleasing to God.

Other announced victories, however, are claimed by default, and reek of emptiness like receiving an A on an examination after having stolen the answer sheet.

The Christian high school student who never appropriated God's promises to help her in her work, and who was undisciplined in her studies which resulted in her failing most of her classes, now declares, "You don't have to worry about me going to college and becoming involved in the drug and sex scene."

The Christian man, whose attempts to control his weight ended in failure, now peers over his stomach and with shortness of breath puffs, "Those sexy women offer no temptation to me. God has given me victory over sex sins."

The college-age girl who so badly botched up her grades she couldn't enroll if she wanted to, the obese saint whose girth is so repulsive even his wife runs, and the gossiper who has no problem being a selective fellowshipper since all equally flee from her venom, may claim victory. But such is not the case. They have through failure in one area of life rendered another area inapplicable.

I don't believe the Lord will reward those who claim victory via failure. We cannot mold God into a being who suits our purpose. *God is God and will remain God regardless of our desire to transform Him into the image most conducive to our comfort.*

His grace is sufficient. While those who have been born again cling to this vital truth, His sufficiency and willingness to forgive our shortcomings does not provide us with license to continue excluding Him from facets of our lives we wish to keep for ourselves. This practice constitutes willful abuse of God's grace.

Minimize Deficiencies

How do we determine which areas of our life we'll turn over to Christ and which ones we won't? I contend that *the more I enjoy the results which come from not turning a particular area of my life over to Christ, the least likely I am to yield it to Him.*

My willingness to turn my tongue over to His control is inversely proportional to the amount of satisfaction I derive from being the center of attraction at a gossip session.

My willingness to bring my appetite under His subjection is inversely proportional to the amount of satisfaction I receive from gobbling mashed potatoes, pizza, and hot fudge sundaes.

If you commit adultery in your mind and heart when you view an attractive person of the opposite sex and immensely enjoy the vicarious gratification you receive, chances are you'll experience great difficulty relinquishing that facet of your life to Him.

Yet an amazing truth surfaces when you finally yield that problem area to Him. *The amount of joy and spiritual energy released in your life is directly proportional to the difficulty and rigorousness of the battle.*

Joy exudes from a person who finally through Christ has conquered the weight problem she's carried for years.

Glory shines from the dad who after committing his temper to Christ has finally found control in times of adversity.

Persons who fail to yield a chosen compartment of their life to Christ and, as a result, dabble in sin and experience failure often gravitate to others having similar failure experiences.

It's as though the guilt is alleviated when we can point the finger to the other losers we surround ourselves with.

Two ways exist to make you feel better about your deficiencies: (1) Make progress towards correcting them or, (2) associate with others having the same or greater deficiencies thereby creating the illusion that you're normal or better off than most.

As a general rule, people tend to condemn others for their deficiencies in areas they feel they have totally conquered.

How often have you heard a "fatty," talk about someone else's obesity, or a gossiper talk about another gossiper, or a non-giver talk of another's failure to tithe? No way do they wish to participate in any discussion which might bring to light their own shortcomings unless through recent success they now consider themselves experts. During this process the condemning person fails to acknowledge his shortcomings in spite of God's instructions to not look for specks in other's eyes when logs exist in their own.

"And so, dear brothers, I plead with you to give your *bodies* to God. Let them be a living sacrifice, holy—the kind he can accept" (Rom. 12:1, *TLB,* italics added).

Billy Graham states in his book *The Holy Spirit,* "This includes every area of our lives. It includes our abilities, our gifts, our possessions, and our families—our minds, wills and emotions. Nothing is excluded. We can hold nothing back. In principle He must control and dominate us in the whole and the part."[2]

When Paul admonishes us to present our bodies to God, he is telling us that God is asking for all of us. Bodies in totality are composed of body, mind and spirit and no part is excluded from this request.

Total Involvement

Presenting our bodies to Him as a "living sacrifice, holy—the kind He can accept" denotes our need to involve Him in every area of our life. If we fail to do so, can the areas we've chosen to exclude Him from ever be truly acceptable to Him? Our humanness (exclusive of His presence and power) would undoubtedly render those areas unacceptable to Him.

I must involve Him in my joy, my family, my thought life, my desires, my relationships with others, my marriage, my children, my parents, my church, my money, my material possessions, my sex life, my fitness program, my health, my heartaches, my joys, my hobbies, my longings, my unsettledness, my shortcomings, my victories and virtually my total existence.

Not to involve Him in every facet of my life creates several problems.

First, it raises questions about the credibility of my faith. If God's involvement in raising my children is deemed necessary, yet I exclude His presence and rightful place in my world of employment, can my faith really be valid? If He adds insight, wisdom, and strength to one undertaking, doesn't it logically follow He'd positively contribute to the other?

Second, it demonstrates my disbelief in the ability of my God. "I can do all things through Him who strengthens me," if believed, certainly merits application of His strength to every area of my life.

Third, it limits my fulfillment. Our self-concept is dependent upon our ability to successfully handle the rigors of life in the manner in which we think we should be able. Christ's involvement in every area insures us of greater success in those areas and greater success increases our fulfillment and makes us feel better about ourselves and Him.

Fourth, it limits my witness. Obvious shortcomings apparent in our lives limit our opportunities to witness. When an observer sees his condition—as an unbeliever—to be as desirable as your condition—as one who claims to be redeemed—what do you have to offer him? "What you are speaks so loud, the world can't hear what you say."

Fifth, I displease the Father. As a father myself I cannot be truly happy when one area of my life stands in disrepair. Regardless of how well things are going at the office, if my daughter is experiencing difficulties at school, happiness flees me.

My heavenly Father is pleased when our lives are in accord with His purpose. When we selectively exclude Him from a segment of our lives, we diminish His happiness and fulfillment.

The Scriptures entreat us to involve God maximally in all areas of our lives. "Do not let any part of your bodies become tools of wickedness, to be used for sinning; *but give yourselves completely to God—every part of you*—for you are back from death and you want to be tools in the hands of God, to be used for his good purposes" (Rom. 6:13, *TLB,* italics added). Can we really justify withholding our thought lives, our family, our desires, our appetite, or any other area from Him?

Jesus states, "If you abide in Me, and My words abide in you, ask whatever you wish, and it shall be done for you" (John 15:7). As it is impossible to abide in a house and leave your leg on the front porch, it is impossible to abide in Jesus Christ and leave any area of your life outside Him. We may say we're abiding in Him but when we're failing to submit segments of our life to Him, our claims lack credibility and echo of emptiness.

Abiding also necessitates obedience (in this case to God's Word and the leading of His Holy Spirit). Even our thought life must be obedient to Christ. "We are destroying speculations and every lofty thing raised up against the knowledge of God, and we are taking every thought captive to the obedience of Christ" (2 Cor. 10:5). How important it is to involve Him in our thought life since our thoughts determine our actions, "As a man thinks so is he" (see Prov. 23:7).

The Lord never asks us to follow His plan without providing an award for our obedience. "Don't copy the behavior and customs of this world, but be a new and different person with a fresh newness in all you do and think. Then you will learn from your own experience how his ways will really satisfy you" (Rom. 12:2, *TLB*).

When we invoke God's involvement only in selected areas of our lives we limit His impact and our fulfillment. By contrast, when every area is laid open to Him, He promises us a fresh newness, satisfaction, and receptivity to hear and supply our needs.

As we cling to certain areas of our lives with clenched fists we rob ourselves of fulfillment, for clenched fists can't be filled. Only when we open our fists and turn our hands and lives upward can He fill our open hands and lives with all His possessions.

The more of our lives we withhold the less room He has to infill us with His blessings.

Lord, in the past I believed that giving you all areas of my life would interfere with the good times I anticipated. Thanks for showing me that to do less, severely limits your ability to fully bless me. I will no longer look upon your presence as a restriction but as an opportunity to live life more abundantly.

Exercise for Understanding

1. List the areas of your life you've not turned over to God.
   a.

   b.

   c.

2. How has holding back part of your life possibly affected your witness?
   a.

   b.

   c.

3. What reasons (other than those discussed) prevent you from opening all areas of your life to God?

4. Describe the feelings which come when, after a struggle, you finally commit an area to Christ.

5. With a confidant, spouse, or trusted friend, make a commitment to faithfully pray about one area of your life you've not been able to commit to God.

Notes

1. Billy Graham, *The Holy Spirit* (Waco, TX: Word Books, 1978), p. 44.
2. Ibid., p. 116.

6
Grading God

"Give ear to my prayer, O God; and do not hide Thyself from my supplication. Give heed to me, and answer me" (Ps. 55:1,2). Just as David did, down through the ages man has wanted God to answer his prayers, yet at times he questioned whether God ignores him.

I have prayed through countless situations and committed numerous requests to God in prayer. Like most children of God I have experienced some miraculous answers, solutions to problematic situations, and been granted undeserved peace in the face of seeming adversity.

There are a number of situations I commit to Him, however, which I perceive as not being answered. These "unanswered" requests somehow loom big on my mind and overshadow the numerous preceding answers I've experienced. I have a tendency to live in the now and the disappointment of the present is greatly amplified. The chapter of life I am currently living in, if it is accompanied by unresolved conflict, erases all the preceding chapters of fulfillment which I may have experienced.

In the absence of an answer or a resolution to a difficult situation, I question my faith and commitment and even raise doubts as to the existence of a caring God.

The overall ledger may read "answered prayers 150—unanswered prayers 3." Yet if one of those three unanswered prayers exists in the here and now, my mental scorecard erases the preceding record and in reality reads "unanswered prayers 1—answered 0."

I've often wondered if the Lord accepts my weighing system, for surely He must agree that some answers to prayer are much more important than others.

I gave Him a +3 for helping me pass that last exam.

I gave Him a +4 for keeping me alert when that boy darted out in front of my car.

Certainly He deserves the full +10 for miraculously curing my friend of cancer.

And a +8 or +9 for pulling the Johnsons' marriage back together.

What audacity! Me taking the liberty of grading God. Yet if I'm honest I must admit I do engage in this practice all too frequently. Imagine me, encumbered by finiteness, trying to evaluate the One who knows no limits.

Is it possible that my system could be faulty? Maybe some of those answers to the seemingly mundane problems are the most potent of all, yet I've been overlooking their significance.

His safekeeping, my family's health, and other highly significant blessings, which I take for granted every day in this world of unforeseen variables and potential tragedies, could comprise the greatest answers of all. Yet I've excluded that from His evaluation and my rating system.

Overlooking the Answer

Most of us have mentally contrived preconceived acceptable answers to our prayers. When we pray for Aunt Doris who's ill, we expect *her to be made well*. When we pray for our daughter who's using drugs, we expect *her to be given strength to "kick" the habit*. When we pray for guidance in our present situation, *we expect Him to provide wisdom allowing us to make the correct decision.*

When God answers our prayers in ways other than those we've visualized, we often feel that He has not answered at all and that He is not concerned about us and our prayer. In this way we attempt to mandate our limitless God to conform to our limited contrived solution, if He is to be deemed a "God who answers prayer."

Shelly was excited about her newly found faith and anxious to share the reality of Christ with her colleagues. Not knowing how to approach Debbie without the risk of turning her off, Shelly prayed, "Lord, give me the opportunity to share my faith with Debbie in a natural, meaningful manner."

Time passed and Shelly had opportunities to discuss her faith with many on the staff, yet actually forgot the request she'd made regarding Debbie.

When we lunched together recently, I asked, "With whom have you shared your faith?"

As Shelly related her contacts and their responses, she suddenly stopped. "Two weeks ago Debbie asked me to begin jogging with her and just now I recognized her request as the answer to my prayer of three months ago."

We rejoiced together.

How many times have you looked back upon a seemingly unanswered prayer only to discover that you had indeed overlooked God's answer? And His wisdom in solving the problem far exceeded the capabilities of your thoughts?

How can I be more sensitive to recognize God's answers to prayer?

As I read the Scriptures and examine the manner in which Christ lived and the action He took in various situations, I become more aware of His unique ministry in meeting my needs. Although I still cannot comprehend His complexity, I become more able to recognize evidences of His answers to my life's problems as I lay them out before Him in prayer.

Recognizing God's Response

Every person sees answered prayer in a different way. Our Bible study group meets on alternate Fridays. The format entails *praise* to God for answered prayer, *prayer, Bible study, discussion* and *personal sharing*. When 18 people have prayed together about a vital concern, there exists a variety of interpretations as to the answer finally received and its significance.

At times I become acutely aware of my inability to see God's answer to our previous request. While I considered one particular prayer unanswered, another group member attested to his unwavering belief that an answer had been received. After examining his explanation and evidence it became obvious that the Holy Spirit had shown him that a unique answer had been given which had passed right over my head. I was looking for an answer to conform to my expectation and was so locked in that when it differed from my blueprint, I failed to recognize it.

On those occasions when I feel my prayers have not received proper consideration, who, if anyone, is to blame? Has God let me down or could it be that shortcomings on my part have lessened the effectiveness of my prayer life? I must examine some key questions.

- Do I have a personal relationship with Christ?
- Have I confessed my sins to Christ in prayer?
- Am I praying with proper motivation?
- Am I persistent in my prayers?
- Am I obedient to Him and His Word?
- Am I seeking His will?
- Am I sensitive to His Holy Spirit to the point where I would recognize His answer even if He laid it out in front of me, or am I fully absorbed in the minutia of everyday life?
- Am I praising the Lord in advance for His answers?

God promises that even when we don't know how to pray, the Holy Spirit translates the desires of our heart to God (see Rom. 8:26). If that is true, the Holy Spirit is the primary resource to solve today's problems.

At times I fail to recognize God's answer to my dilemma until the situation becomes past history. The benefits and insights derived are in arrears. Mom continually prayed for Dad's salvation and deeply desired that he come to church with her. Finally he promised. But on Sunday the furnace malfunctioned. She was deeply grieved that God had allowed this to happen after her prayers were finally answered regarding Dad's willingness to attend. Distraught, she began to gather her purse and Bible while herding her three kids into the 1947 Ford.

Almost across the threshold, she decided to take a radio down to where Dad was repairing the furnace. Turning the radio on to WMBI, Mom mounted the steps and left for church. The radio evangelist, led by the Holy Spirit, was sensitized to Dad's need. "You may be the Sunday School superintendent of one of the largest churches in the city (and he was), you may be a successful business man (and he was)" and he continued the barrage as if he intimately knew Dad.

Dad accepted the Lord as his personal Saviour that morning while Mom assumed her prayers to be unanswered. Later that day, they rejoiced together.

I have become convinced that the answers to prayer may be proportionate to my closeness to the Lord, to my faithfulness and alertness in prayer, to my expressed belief in His ability to perform and to whether I view prayer and God from a negative or positive orientation.

Dwelling upon His goodness to us as demonstrated through answered prayer and resolutions to our problem situations will cause us to praise and glorify Him.

Glorifying Him is to be our chief end, for all things (including us) were made for His Glory.

When we glorify Him He is blessed and our fulfillment and sensitivity to His Holy Spirit are increased, providing us with new awareness and increased perception of His answers and goodness to us.

A Point of View

Often the attitude with which I view a situation determines to a large extent what I will ultimately see. If my approach is one of negativism, I'll find an abundance to criticize. If my approach is positively based, I'll find good. We possess the uncanny ability of discovering what we expect to discover. "I've already made up my mind, don't confuse me with the facts," is apropos since the positive or negative pedestal from which I render a judgment, often overrides the weighty conclusive evidence which comes forth.

As a principal of a school I make it a point to greet the parents of newly enrolled students. On occasion I've had a parent react to my welcome by stating, "We have big concerns about sending our daughter to this school. We've heard the kids in this neighborhood are tough, and we're concerned about our daughter's safety and the quality of education she'll receive."

When this scene has been screened, I am at once aware that no amount of explanation on my part will change the parent's attitude. He is operating from a negative base and will microscopically examine every function we undertake in an effort to prove his preconceived conclusions valid. His negativism often rubs off on his child who naturally didn't want to leave her former school anyway. With Mom, Dad, and child now negatively oriented, the chances of a positive school experience are slim indeed.

By contrast, I'm delighted to welcome parents who express, "I don't know much about your school, but we'll expect the best." They then proceed to get involved and look for good things to happen. When they possess a positive orientation, positive experiences generally occur.

It's no different with God and our perception of answered prayer.

If my perception of God is of one who is standing over me with a big stick waiting to zap me into line while saying "I told you so," I'm viewing Him from a negative base and will seek to substantiate His coldness and lack of concern and empathy by pointing to His shortcomings and inabilities to meet my needs as demonstrated through "unanswered prayer." I usually find what *I'm seeking because my desire to be proven right, overshadows my ability to be objective*.

Conversely, if I positively view God as love and as One who desires the best for me, I'll be more sensitive to His work in my life. And I will be more able to perceive the answers to prayer which, without my positive orientation, might have gone unnoticed.

I must pray with a positive attitude then positively expect my prayers to be answered. I must open-mindedly and positively examine my circumstances to identify and acknowledge His answers. Then I must praise Him for His faithfulness. Only when we proceed from a positive base do we receive all that God has for us. Then we will have the joy He intends us to have. "Ask, and you will receive, that your joy may be made full" (John 16:24).

Double Standard

My double standard at times amazes even me. Slipping between the covers I begin, "Dear God, thanks for your Son Jesus and the salvation I have through Him. I ask you to forgive me for the impure thoughts I had at work today, the time I struck out in anger and told my daughter 'go play on the freeway,'" and—(long pause)—"z-z-z-z."

Two minutes later I turn to my right side, jolting me back to a conscious state, and continue, "Where was I God? Oh, yes, I praise you for my family and Lord—z-z-z-z."

A car pulling into the driveway next door momentarily awakens me and I continue, "And Lord, about the difficult situations. Please give me the wisdom to—z-z-z-z."

If the Lord wasn't omniscient He'd check heaven's antennas to see why I keep fading in and fading out.

The horrendous clanging of the alarm clock two feet from my ear jolts me to my feet to begin a new day. Later, I share with the Christian friend with whom I work, "How blessed my daily devotions are."

Can you imagine how long a human relationship would remain vital if 80 percent of the time, while you conversed with your friend, you slipped off into dreamland and left him waiting? But, I expect God to be there and hang on my every word. And more than that, I expect God to perform wonders and treat my needs with earth-shaking importance even though I can't stay awake long enough to talk to Him about them. Beyond that, if He doesn't answer as I think He should I often attribute the failure to Him while assuming no responsibility myself.

I become convicted when I read, "Devote yourselves to prayer, keeping alert in it with an attitude of thanksgiving" (Col. 4:2).

I do not believe I'm being fair with God—to question His abilities and faithfulness in regard to answered prayer—when I have an inept prayer life.

Each person must work out a system for himself which allows him to be alert and thoughtful in prayer if he is to truly experience God's potential through his prayer life. Since drifting off into sleep is a problem with me, I've incorporated a dual program of physical and spiritual fitness.

God has blessed me with the uncanny ability to fall instantly and deeply asleep whenever my head and shoulders rest anywhere between a 45-degree angle and a flat surface. Because of this, if my prayer life was to be effective, I had to make allowances for my blessing.

Having noticed my mind to be most alert during exercise, I've reserved my jogging time for time alone with Christ in prayer. My routine goes something like this:

Lap 1—Praise God

Lap 2—Confess and ask forgiveness

Lap 3—Thank Him for provisions and blessings (time for itemization)

Lap 4—Dottie

Lap 5—Dawn

Lap 6—Danelle

Lap 7—Denise

Lap 8—Me (itemize concerns and needs)

Lap 9—Friends (requests)

Lap 10—Opportunities

Lap 11—Body of believers

Lap 12—Thanks for expected answers and increased sensitivity through the Holy Spirit to recognize those answers.

Lap 13 & 14—(Cool off while walking), cover miscellaneous areas that don't fit specific categories.

There are those who would criticize this method of prayer life, but I guess I'm a pragmatist. I've never yet fallen asleep jogging. The freshly oxygenated blood pouring through my brain adds clarity to my communion with the God I love.

In addition, I have to believe that God is pleased anytime I or any believer fellowships with Him in prayer. When He said to "pray without ceasing," He didn't exclude the jogging track, the pool, driving the freeway (with your eyes open!), lying on the back lawn, cutting the grass or any other activity or location. He must not be tied to form or tradition but really must be interested in the sincere expression of my heart.

There are few things to equal the feeling I derive from running and talking with God while I watch the sun set or the approaching darkness bring the stars into prominence. This practice has converted the drudgery of exercise into delight.

God has promised, "Call to Me, and I will answer you, and I will tell you great and mighty things, which you do not know" (Jer. 33:3). Since He's promised to answer me, I believe He will. "He has inclined His ear to me, therefore I shall call upon Him as long as I live" (Ps. 116:2).

The Word of God declares, "Until now you have asked for nothing in My name; ask, and you will receive, that your joy may be made full" (John 16:24). If one condition of living in joy is asking the Lord for His provisions and blessings, here's one Christian who won't quit.

Please, Lord, sensitize me with your Holy Spirit, so my joy may be made full as I ask for things in your name, then allow me to be perceptive enough to recognize your answers and apply them fully to my life.

Exercise for Understanding

Post a monthly calendar in a private, prominent place.

1. On the calendar note in the appropriate daily squares specific requests you make to the Lord.

2. As answers to your prayers become evident, record the answers on the date they're revealed to you.

3. Draw a line through those requests as answers become evident.

4. Review the calendar at month's end. This visual awareness of abundant answers will confirm a high percentage of prayer effectiveness.

5. At month's end, carry forward to first of next month any requests that God has not yet answered.

6. Summarize year-end totals and you'll be amazed at His average.

7
Modeling Misery

When we adults get caught up in the busyness of life we often forget we're in the modeling profession. Years after our kids have left the roost, we'll notice that they react to various situations in much the same way we did. When we observe ourselves reflected in their negative actions, it's "blah" time again.

If you are a parent you may implement every joy strategy we've discussed so far, and some we've yet to mention, and still live with a heavily-burdened heart when your children are experiencing severe problems.

Regardless of our children's ages, marital status, or place of residence, parental love, loyalty, and depth of feeling run so deeply we can hardly have joy when they're miserable.

What we as parents fail to realize and hate to admit is that we must actually lay claim to much of our children's misery.

Most of us would agree that each person at the age of accountability must own the responsibility for his own decisions. How then as parents do we contribute to our children's problems thus diminishing their chance of joy and ours?

Do As I Say . . .
A sizeable number of parents wrongly assume that our verbal instructions comprise the majority of our children's

education. However, many habits and practices are not verbally taught but are learned through observing parents and others whom young people respect as models.

This truth is so beautifully stated in the words to a song entitled, "What You Are."

> What you are speaks so loud
> The world can't hear what you say,
> They're looking at your walk
> Not listening to your talk
> They're judging by your actions every day.
> Don't believe, that you'll deceive
> By claiming that you've never known
> They'll accept what they see
> And know you to be—
> They'll judge by your life alone.[1]

From the earliest toddler stage, Bobby picks up his lunch pail and pretends to leave for work to be a fireman just like Dad. When asked by his kindergarten teacher what he wants to be, Bobby dons his fire helmet and describes in detail Dad's duties.

Sally washes her play dishes, pretends to scrub the floor and practices her ironing on the kitchen table. She has, even at this early age, learned well from Mom's model.

We may lecture eloquently to our children about a healthy attitude towards work yet regularly come home in an angry mood complaining about how much we hate our jobs. Our actions will likely negate all our talk and we should not be surprised when later we discover that our children possess the same sour attitude towards their jobs which we've displayed towards ours.

Many a father and mother who've terminated their marriage are deeply troubled when years later all their children have failed to maintain a lasting relationship. They've effectively modeled "quitting" and their sons and daughters learned well how to bail out rather than work it out. Have you ever noticed that in many cases divorce seems to be familial?

If you have occasion to observe a young couple where the man unselfishly pitches in to accomplish housework and other duties related to living, invariably his dad was thoughtful around the house and secure in his manhood as well. Positive and negative modeling has a lasting effect upon lives.

Recently, Danelle, my 11-year-old, and I drove to the market together to pick up a few groceries. We talked of many things as we stood behind several carts patiently waiting our turn to check out. (Do you also have a way of selecting the slowest line?)

Our groceries were totalled and I handed the checker a twenty-dollar bill. While counting the change and placing the bills across my outstretched palm, I noticed she had given me five dollars more than she should have. I handed her the extra bill and kidded her about the inadequacies of the "new math."

While loading the groceries into our trunk, Danelle exclaimed, "Boy, Dad, are you honest. You could have really ripped them off."

That simple incident, and a similar one which occurred a week later in the local cleaners, was God's way of reinforcing and reminding me of the awesome responsibility we have of living honest lives before our kids. Had Danelle seen me keep the extra change, and rip off the system, all my exhortations to be honest would have been worthless.

Some claim modeling has a more pronounced effect upon the very young, which may well be the case since "parents" and "idols" are often synonymous in early childhood. We must take care, however, to refrain from minimizing the effects of modeling during the preteen and teen years. We often assume that modeling has little effect on our adolescents because of the somewhat rebellious attitude we sense in them. We don't realize that this attitude represents their attempts to achieve the much sought after independence. Where their actions and attitudes, at times, seem to demonstrate out-and-out defiance and are usually in direct contradiction to those of their parents, shortly after they achieve independence a large percentage return to adopt the same mores they contradicted only a short time before.

A family where Mom and Dad are grossly overweight and regularly gorge themselves from the dinner hour until they struggle to pull the comforter over their rotund frames, will likely produce kids who adopt their same unhealthy eating patterns. While tendencies towards obesity are somewhat familial, obesity can and is often caused because children adopt the poor eating habits modeled by Mom, Dad, or both.

Reverse Modeling

We must also acknowledge, however, that parental models are sometimes so despicable to the children that they adopt uncompromising opposite roles and stringently adhere to them their entire life.

My friend, Tony, had an alcoholic father who was frequently stoned out of his mind. The family suffered from insufficient provisions as Dad squandered much of the paycheck at the local tavern before finding his way home. Observing his dad and the hardship alcoholism placed on the family, Tony, as a teenager, vowed never to allow alcohol to affect him or those he loved. He developed a hatred for everything alcohol represented. Tony is now middle age and has yet to allow a drop of alcohol to enter his system or his home.

Joe was a sensitive ninth grader who, compared to his classmates, spent an inordinate amount of time offering his services around school. When I questioned him regarding his early arrival and late departure each day, he broke down and described the beatings he and his mother had taken at the hands of his dad who had recently been released from his job.

At the close of our conversation we talked about adversity and whether anything good could ever come of it. Joe thought for a moment, then said, ''I just know that when I'm down on myself or something bad has happened to me, I'm never going to take it out on anyone, especially the people I'm supposed to love.''

Some may feel this occasional tendency for children to rebel against the despicable parental traits gives license for parents to live ungodly lives—''My kids will come out O.K. anyway.''

As God warned us not ''to continue in sin that grace may increase'' (Rom. 6:1) we parents must heed the same warning lest our children adopt all our negative behaviors with the resulting devastating consequences.

We have two choices as parents. We may, with the help and strength the Lord has promised, live as exemplary a life as possible, or live totally unto our own desires without regard to the example we're setting for our children.

If we forsake our responsibility to positively model for our children, our chances of total joy are severely diminished. Later in life, as we view our grown children experiencing troubles which may have been avoided had we fulfilled our obligations, any joy we could be experiencing will be lessened.

If we relinquish our opportunity to model, the opportunity will often be seized by a peer group, another individual or cult leader who may choose to model traits we consider extremely negative.

Modeling Godliness

Isn't parental modeling less important in the lives of Christians?

If you've accepted the Lord as your Saviour you were taught to adopt Jesus Christ alone as your model. We were told, "Men will always fail you, but Jesus never will."

This is indeed true. However, to use Jesus Christ as our example we must read about Him regularly and study His attributes, mode of operation, and reactions to the pressures of life. Since the majority of young Christians lack discipline in studying the Word, our parents, and later our peers, assume the number 1 model role by default.

The Christian parent has the distinct privilege of living a Christlike life before his children so that they may see Christ through him. Is there a higher calling than living a life through which your own children view Jesus Christ?

Often we as Christians fail this task by parading holier-than-thou perfection attitudes. When we display this attitude to our kids, they feel inferior and hesitate to attempt new tasks for fear of failing to match their parents' perfection. When we display this attitude to non-Christians, instead of openly admitting our problems and fallibility, we establish a phony standard and to them become unapproachable.

Let's be honest enough to apologize to our kids and others when we're wrong. Modeling humanness is often as important as modeling godliness for it establishes our credibility.

It would be a mistake to assume that faithfulness in modeling on the part of parents will always mean the children will be well adjusted, moral and turned on to life. My purpose in discussing modeling is not to lay a guilt trip on parents whose kids have gone astray. Some model well and live exemplary lives, yet external and internal pressures on their children cause deviations in behavior and resultant heartaches. We can be sure, however, that faithful modeling will increase their chances and ours of fulfillment and happiness.

If we indeed wish to model Jesus Christ, we must first realize our human limitations, regularly read His Word (to see how He responded to situations we daily encounter), pray (for His strength and guidance in living a Christlike life), and be sensitive to the Holy Spirit's leading and direction.

The apostle Paul realized the importance of modeling when he wrote to the church at Philippi, "The things you have learned and received and heard and seen in me, practice these things; and the God of peace shall be with you" (Phil. 4:9).

There is no easy way to be an effective model, but the consequences of failing to do so will keep us from the joy God intended for our lives.

Lord, may I be faithful to the task of modeling. And may your blessings allow me to say, with the apostle John, "I have no greater joy than this, to hear of my children walking in the truth" (3 John 4).

Exercise for Understanding

1. List the three most important attributes you think you should model as a parent. After each one, describe the most recent incident which allowed you to reinforce it.

   a.

   b.

   c.

2. In case you think you've arrived, ask your mate to tape record your at-home conversation without your knowledge. Then take time in private to listen to yourself to determine whether you're modeling effectively. What did you discover?

3. Reflect upon the human model who most positively influenced your life. Describe the attributes you respected most highly in that person.

Note

1. H.S. Leaman, "What You Are." Copyright 1922. Renewal 1950 by Juanita Leaman Gottschling. Assigned to Singspiration, Inc. All rights reserved. Used by permission.

8
Choosing Sides

Tonight we had dinner with David and Marilyn. Midway through our five-hour dinner, our conversation turned to past and present evangelists and their impact upon our lives.

As each name was brought up the reaction was mixed:

"Kathryn Kuhlman, too dramatic."

"Jim Bakker, too loud and emotional."

"Jimmy Swaggart, too much a showman."

"Oral Roberts, too enterprising."

One by one the roll was called and comments were shared. Each evangelist had been a blessing to some of us, yet the same person evoked a negative response to others of us.

Could the Lord be telling me through that experience that I should be noncritically supportive of His servants regardless of how they personally appeal to me, since God seems to be blessing them and all seem to meet a need for some segment of our populace?

I believe His message to me that evening was, "John, support whomever proclaims my Word, for it takes all kinds of servants to reach all kinds of people."

In one respect most Christians are no different from the majority of the unredeemed. We all love heroes and favorites and although we of the Body of Christ are schooled to fix our eyes on Christ alone and only emulate His example, many can't repress the urge to pedestal certain people who meet our needs or possess qualities we respect. After all, we've been spoon-fed from preschool times to revere George Washington, Abraham Lincoln and others who've found their way into the school curriculum.

When later we become independent thinkers our hero-selection process is usually determined by our interests or some intense need met by those we've adopted.

Hero Worship

Dottie was a young housewife who felt stifled and repressed. She resented being saddled with two demanding children who monopolized her time. Every time she started any project she was interrupted by a child who needed her attention that instant. She felt trapped.

Simultaneous with Dottie's situation, Gloria Steinam thrust the woman's liberation movement into national prominence. Gloria's philosophy offered Dottie a way out. She could hire a sitter and go to work and experience the same fulfillment as her husband.

Gloria met a need in Dottie's life and became her personal heroine.

President John Kennedy was a hero to millions as they saw in him many admirable qualities they felt were lacking in their own lives. His sense of humor, good looks, intelligence, bubbling personality, and ability to make the tough decision won him a place in many hearts. He was personally responsible for the term "charisma" becoming a household word.

The Christian sector adopts heroes as well.

Billy Graham, Oral Roberts, and others have for a variety of reasons captured the hearts of countless Christians. I'm one who doesn't disagree with the practice of Christians adopting heroes. Rightness and wrongness of having heroes is a matter of degree. When I worship my hero or determine my beliefs solely on the basis of my hero maintaining his credibility and living as I think he should, am I wrong?

Sure, I've heard the warnings. "Keep your eyes fixed solely on Christ, because He'll never disappoint you, but man will falter, stumble and fail."

While I know the message in this warning is true, I believe many Christians could profit by developing a deep respect for other Christians and adopting them as heroes or standard-bearers.

So they fail, big deal. I respect David, "a man after God's own heart," and can't wait to embrace Peter. They're two of the heroes of my faith; yet one committed adultery and the other denied my Lord three times. Their failures attest to their humanness and I'm human and will fail. That somehow increases our camaraderie.

While I'm trying to become more like Jesus Christ, I find it easier to look to a person who isn't part of the Godhead and try to determine what makes his life more victorious than mine.

The danger in the Christian adopting the look-only-at-Christ concept is that he rejects what he could learn from other Christians, since they're only human. However, he should respect those who apparently have had more success (spiritually) in handling areas which are problems for him.

Should I not have learned from Paul? Should Peter's failures and victories, and reckless enthusiasm be disregarded since they failed?

Judging Saints

I have found strength, encouragement, and assistance through the lives of Jim Dobson, C.S. Lewis, Corrie ten Boom, Keith Miller, and numerous other lesser known Christians. I respect them greatly and even consider them heroes. My life has been enriched through their work and ministries.

Yet our human heroes will from time to time fall and

when they do we Christians sometimes reek of piousness. We're enthused when a leader contributes to our lives and sing his praises from the housetops. But as soon as his conduct seems questionable to us, we loudly condemn him or at least banish him from our list of credible contributors instead of supporting him through prayer during his struggles.

Keith Miller's book *Taste of New Wine* was the vehicle which lessened the phoniness of many believers while allowing new honesty and openness to characterize their relationship with God and others. My life and lives of my friends and countless others were deepened as a result of Keith's book and subsequent works.

But then Keith's marriage went awry, he married a divorced woman, and lo and behold, a segment of the Christian populace thought they could no longer identify with him. Publications questioned his functional effectiveness in evangelical circles. Some Christian acquaintances of mine even doubted the credibility of his previous works and questioned his ability to minister in the future.

Christians were ready to collectively throw out the baby with the bath water.

Keith's works have blessed me. I learned from *Taste of New Wine* and gained enormous insights from *Please Love Me*, written after his remarriage. Had I jumped on the bandwagon which said, "Keith failed, he couldn't keep his marriage together; therefore he's no use for me," I would have missed some concise and beautiful truths that ministered to my spirit.

It's always interesting to observe a Christian who supports a particular cause for numerous years, yet drops his support cold turkey when a member on the staff of that ministry veers slightly from the supporter's criteria of Christian behavior.

I ask you, can we learn from others' struggles? Can

well-meaning Christians experience divorce? Can a Christian commit sin, ask forgiveness, and then continue to be used of God? I believe they can and I will neither disregard their ministry prior to their "failures" nor will I preclude the possibility of their subsequent works and life ministering to me in the future.

Maturing as a Christian is a continual refining process. As we learn through our trials and burdens we can more astutely assist other people passing through similar deep waters.

Please, brother, don't exclude me from sharing my life with you just because I've stumbled, and I'll reciprocate by being receptive to your life regardless of your trials and setbacks.

We need each other.

Lord, even those saints I hold in high esteem will occasionally fall and stumble as I do. When that happens, keep me open still to what their words and lives are saying. Give me a spirit of support to all those who truly minister in your name, regardless of my personal preference.

Exercise for Understanding

1. Do you agree or disagree with the following statements?

	agree	disagree
a. Being critical of a minister can affect that person's ministry to others.	☐	☐
b. A Christian who is critical of his pastor has an obligation to keep his feelings private.	☐	☐
c. A Christian is obligated to share his criticism when he believes it's valid.	☐	☐
d. Criticism should always be constructive.	☐	☐

2. If a talented Christian with a ministry falls into sin, should he be treated any differently from the "average" Christian? Why or why not?

3. Is someone faithfully and successfully ministering for Christ more apt to fall into sin? Why or why not?

4. How does Matthew 6:14 apply? "For if you forgive men for their transgressions, your heavenly Father will also forgive you."

9
Surrendering to Conflict

Nobody is exempt from criticism (constructive or otherwise), disappointments or adversities. They are as much a part of life as the inevitability of death and taxes.

Yet, while some people can handle criticisms, disappointments and adversities with minimal disruption, others respond to them with an extended case of the blahs.

Handling Criticism

Recent discussions at church and my place of employment have dealt with the necessity of being open and honest if relationships are to grow. The conversation usually swells to incorporate the necessity of being able to accept criticism while determining which facets of the criticism are justified and, if applied, could improve relationships or personal effectiveness. Criticism that is deemed of no particular consequence could then be discarded.

I talk a great game plan, but this very weekend I had an opportunity to practice what I preach and miserably failed the test.

Ironically, I don't even recall the exact word exchange that precipitated the charges my wife brought to my attention. But somewhere within the exchange I was directly reminded that from our marriage day I've had hundreds of plans that would improve our plight and allow us to gain financial independence. In general, the conclusion was that I had followed through with very few of these life-changing plans.

I was even encouraged to refrain from sharing any of my dreams or schemes from now on, until some of them are implemented and could be tested, touched or felt.

Imagine not wanting to be privy to the great workings of a creative mind?

Hurt is an understated word and falls far short of describing my condition after fielding those ego blows. I thought of all the great retorts but, somehow, as I attempted to verbalize them, the truth of the criticism seemed to render them inconsequential.

Frantically searching my mind for facts to refute her allegations, I was disturbed to uncover only two dreams, out of many, that were ever carried to fruition. We didn't have a McDonald's franchise, Fotomat, bookstore, worm farm, rental agency, real estate office, counseling center, or any of the numerous dreams destined to enrich our lives.

By virtue of sharing my many enthusiastic dreams, I was guilty of manipulating my wife's feelings. As I vividly portrayed my newest venture, her hopes would build to a great crescendo only to wane to nothingness when I failed to complete my energetic plans.

Questions ricocheted in my mind. Was I really using my ill-planned schemes to play games with the emotions and stability of my family? Were my kids experiencing some upheaval as they listened to my projects that involved possible relocations and different employment? We had resided in the same community for 16 years, yet maybe family stability isn't produced by remaining in the same geographical area but is the result of knowing that Dad is happy and fulfilled in his work and we needn't be anxious about moving and establishing new relationships at his every whim.

Maturity doesn't preclude long-range goals and excitement about dreams and the future. But these visions and plans must be tempered with common sense and the constant knowledge that other lives (especially the young) are vastly dependent upon decisions made.

I reflected on my responsibility as a parent. If I can't set an example by demonstrating optimism and thankfulness in my present circumstances, how will I ever credibly deal with my youngster who seems to exude dissatisfaction?

Lord, help me realize that if I truly am spiritually mature, I must find a way to curb my unsettledness so those around me are not adversely affected.

I'm not asking for the impossible. Paul proclaimed, "I have learned to be content in whatever circumstances I am" (Phil. 4:11).

Rising above the hassles and emotional highs and lows of everyday life to fulfillment and acceptance is no easy task. Christians are just as susceptible to the pressure cooker as are non-Christians. But I must be sensitive to the fact that my performance affects the lives and performances of others. My apparent unsettledness and negativism are not conducive to anyone around me performing to their optimum capabilities.

As I examined my life, words and actions, I discovered I was often guilty of conveying, verbally or without ever uttering a word, my dissatisfaction to those nearby. It's important to plan ahead. Doesn't the Scripture encourage us to forget those things which are behind and reach forward to what lies ahead? (See Phil. 3:13.)

Yet some of us dwell on the future (as a solution to our problems or the answer to bettering our situation) to such an extent that we say to others who associate with us, "I'm really miserable and dissatisfied with present circumstances and drastically in need of change."

By conveying this attitude we raise questions in the minds of our loved ones, "Am I a contributing factor to Dad's dissatisfaction?'' These questions indicate that they have doubts about their self-worth.

At times our family recognizes our lack of contentment, but we try to hide it from those outside the family. We put on an I've-got-it-all-together display. Because of this attitude our family sees us as hypocrites and our credibility is lessened.

A fine line exists between looking forward constructively and looking forward excessively, rendering ourselves inefficient in the present. Too much ''futurizing'' results in lessening efficiency on the job, preoccupation and dissatisfaction around the home, and the inability to deal effectively with our present situation.

When my wife first accused me of this charge, I was unable to support my defense with facts at hand; so I inwardly fumed. ''She doesn't appreciate me at all. Doesn't she know how highly respected I am at work? Others think I'm effective, yet she criticizes and attacks my very credibility.'' At the very moment she criticized me, my dear wife left the realm of lover, companion, and mother of my children to assume the role of villain.

In the past, my course of action would have been to shut her out of my life, give her the silent treatment while I wallowed in self-pity and hurt. That'll do the trick I schemed. Soon she'll make her entrance apologizing and begging my forgiveness.

But, if I'm to grow, I must recognize the truth which she and others forthrightly point out to me and apply it to my life. I must also recognize the fact that to convey honest expressions of concern to another is a difficult task and often requires a great deal of love.

Thanks, dear, for caring enough to let me know about the things in my life which bother you. I trust I'll be faithful to you and others in the same way.

The Sunday message was excellent and the fellowship

blessed but the greatest growth this weekend began in what seemed a spiteful way, yet emerged a blessing.

Evaluating Disappointment

Friday night found me making a list of the myriad of chores I was going to accomplish around my house the next day.

Winter had taken a severe toll on our acre. The heaviest California rainfall in over a hundred years had prevented me from keeping up with the (now waist high) weeds and widely scattered debris.

The weedeater was repaired, tuned up, the gas was mixed and I was ready to go. Surely by noon I could have that orchard mowed down and would be able to proceed with numbers 2-10 on my list of chores.

What a sense of relief I would have on Saturday night with all those jobs behind me.

Eight o'clock A.M.—I pulled the starting cord and the engine roared. I could just picture the weeds being mowed down to the nubs as the weedeater's power was unleashed. I lit into that first bank of weeds and all went as planned for two minutes. As I reached to depress the buttons necessary to release additional inches of the cutting material, the buttons failed to respond. They were frozen.

I pushed and pushed and even whacked on them with the head of a hammer, but to no avail. Not having the proper tool to disassemble the head, I knew I must take the green-machine back to the shop that repaired it.

"Steamed" wasn't vivid enough to describe my mental state. I threw that machine into the trunk of my car and promptly drove to the repair shop.

A number of people were waiting to be served but certainly they could understand my abruptness as I plopped the machine down on the counter, publicly calling attention to the shop's incapable help.

Politely and promptly (how else when the customer is 6'8" tall and weighs 250 pounds) the repairman found the problem. I stood over him to make certain he performed well this time. After all, this shop had already caused me to fall behind in my work schedule and I was beginning to feel pressure within.

Home again, I fired up the machine and the next half hour went just as I had planned.

Reaching down to clear the weeds wrapped around the head of the machine, I was fit to be tied when I noticed the cutting material had recessed into the machine. This would mean another delay and this orchard would take forever to clear.

Frantically searching for a tool to disassemble the spool cover, I snapped "no" to my youngest daughter's request without ever fully hearing it. Doesn't she knew that everyone pays when Dad's plans go awry? After all, she's obligated to love me no matter how I act.

Forty-five minutes were consumed threading that elusive piece of nylon thread out of that machine.

Back in the orchard I marched, knowing even to get to number 5 on my priority job list I must work faster and more efficiently.

Two minutes later the nylon had again disappeared and so had any semblance of patience on my part. With great restraint I kept from throwing the green-machine into the blue sky and watching it crash into the black earth.

Was I ever ticked off! I was non-responsive to my family, irritable, and bothered by the knowledge that next Saturday would again find me far behind schedule, strapped to that no-good machine.

God, how could you let this happen to me?

Sunday I found out that a friend was readmitted to the hospital. Her bout with cancer has lasted for months and months with the pain so excruciating at times she passes out or must be sedated. Yet she talks about God's peace and ministers to all who go to minister to her. She has accepted her plight with the perfect knowledge that God has the power to heal her or take her to Himself. She declares openly that she is ready for either option and awaits His decision.

That Sunday, others came to mind who were hurting and whose lives seemed to be torn asunder.

Suddenly the weedeater problems of the previous day were put in the proper perspective. How could I let such an insignificant incident temporarily dismantle my life for a 12-hour period?

My weekend experience vividly demonstrated to me the ease with which I get caught up in the disappointing experiences that affect me. I must grow from selfishness to the place where I can see disappointments in the total perspective of life, if I am ever to minister to those who at this time are really experiencing suffering or disappointments. I must help them sense, through the Holy Spirit, that their present sufferings are not worth comparing with the glory that will be revealed to them (see Rom. 8:18).

And if their real sufferings are not worth comparing, I'm embarrassed at allowing my picayune weekend experience to detrimentally affect my life in any way.

Coping with Adversity

"There are no accidents in the life of a Christian," said Dave about something that occurred only the night before.

"I had finished a long, tiring day of work before retiring. Shortly after falling asleep, my wife and I heard this loud rumble followed by a noisy, destructive crash in the field next to our house.

"I couldn't imagine what had happened. Lois sat straight up in bed and, although I longed to go back to sleep, her concern compelled me to investigate the circumstances.

"Lo and behold, as I checked my vehicles on my hilly,

country driveway, one of my trucks was missing.

"Tying the rumbling sound together with the missing truck, I mentally created the picture of someone stealing the truck; but why would he drive it through the field rather than following the road?

"The breaking of dawn answered my questions. Somehow our truck began to roll down the rough terrain. I guess we'll never know if someone was tampering with it and released the brake as a prank, or was planning to steal it when he lost control, panicked and jumped out to avoid injury. Anyhow, the rampaging truck, with a full head of steam, crashed into the house at the bottom of the hill.

"Amazingly, the truck broke through the garage and came to rest alongside their parked car, inflicting a single small scratch on it.

"Walking down the hill to survey the damage, my irritation began to swell. Why this? Somebody down there could be injured or killed; the truck likely is inoperable which will affect our work schedule; the repairs will be costly and I just don't have time to fool with this whole mess.

"Then the Spirit of the Lord communicated with my spirit saying, 'Dave, aren't you one of God's children? If you are, you must accept the fact that there are no "accidents" in your life.' "

When Dave related his experience to me, including the mental process of irritation swelling to anger and resentment, I identified with him on a deep level; for all too frequently I find myself in a similar frame of mind. Yet Dave discovered the secret of accepting all occurrences in his life as planned by the Master.

You may question the validity of a person being able to have this level of trust in God. Wasn't he just saying that in public and brooding in private?

Unequivocally, no. My wife and I spent the weekend following the incident with Dave and Lois. Their spirits were sweet as they shared their lives with never a mention of the near tragedy. The joy in their lives was obviously genuine.

What an important principle I learned through Dave's experience.

Accepting the adversities which enter my life as planned events, designated to shape me into the person God wants me to be, supplants the negative feelings with the positive joy of the Lord.

Poppycock! you say?

No, it's spiritual.

"For from Him and through Him and to Him are all things. To Him be the glory forever" (Rom. 11:36).

Either I accept the Scriptures as His infallible Word or my faith is worthless. If I accept it, this verse tells me that "all things" whether blessing or adversity are "from Him and through Him."

What implications! The adversity I experience takes on new light when I view it as being placed in my life by the God I love. If I accept it on that basis, I then have the right to give it back to Him and praise Him for allowing the anticipated growth to occur in my life.

That's not the easiest thing to do, but consider the alternatives: (1) you could curse God for allowing the adversity to occur; (2) you could allow anger and resentment to eat at your innards and jeopardize your mental, emotional and physical health; (3) you could write the whole negative occurrence off as lady luck.

Notice. None of the three options did a thing to eliminate or ward off the adversity. It has occurred and its effects will now be amplified by the devastating and embroiled feelings you harbor within.

First Corinthians 8:6 says, "Yet for us there is but one God, the Father, from whom are all things, and we exist for Him; and one Lord, Jesus Christ, through whom are all things, and we exist through Him." How much better to view adversity in the light of this verse and bask in His goodness for bringing us through the circumstances and seeking His purpose in placing these events in our life.

The appropriate question at this point isn't, "Why me, Lord?" but becomes, "What do you want to teach me through this, Lord?"

This attitude is difficult to develop even when God is Lord of your life, but it's nigh unto impossible to implement if you don't accept Him in that capacity.

I've got so far to go in this area of my Christian experience. When adversity enters my life I question: Don't you care, God? Why did you allow this to happen to me? What have I done to deserve this? Bitterness at times swells to the level that it immobilizes me in the present.

I can remember leaning over my mom's casket, eyes swollen with tears, saying, "That's not fair, God, she's only 69 and such a beautiful person." Shortly thereafter I realized my bitterness as destructive and self-defeating.

At that point, the Spirit of the Lord directed me to ask forgiveness for my bitterness and offer thanksgiving for being privileged to have a godly mom for as long as I did.

I've carried the negative barrage to the point that I've actually questioned my faith. Then great remorse fills my heart when Job comes to my remembrance. The worst adversity I've ever suffered could not compare with the losses Job suffered; yet he hung in there and faithfully sought God's purpose even when his wife and dearest friends were advising him to curse God and die. Job was blessed abundantly for his faithfulness.

Lord, I'm so embarrassed at my inability to put into practice the procedures you've given for converting travesty to joy.

Let me with Paul live the realization that "God causes all things to work together for good to those who love God, to those who are called according to His purpose" (Rom. 8:28).

Lord, thanks for Dave and his example. Thanks that through his acceptance of adversity as part of your plan I could observe joy flowing into his life.

May you work in my life that I may lay claim to my share of your joy as you allow me to experience trials and burdens.

Exercise for Understanding

1. How did you respond to the most recent criticism that was directed towards you?

   a. Immediate response:

   b. Feelings by the next morning:

2. Do you agree or disagree with the following statements?

	agree	disagree
a. It is better to avoid criticizing others, even if you think they need it, for fear of offending someone.	☐	☐
b. Criticism cannot take place without negative effects.	☐	☐
c. Criticism always hurts a relationship.	☐	☐
d. We have an obligation to offer criticism to those we care about.	☐	☐
e. Learning to accept criticism is an important ingredient in good mental health.	☐	☐
f. Often, criticism indicates caring.	☐	☐

3. Recall the most recent adversity that affected your life. Write down three feelings you associate with this occasion.
   a.

   b.

   c.

4. During the time you harbored these feelings, what effect did this adversity have on your life?

5. Give a personal example in which you felt the Lord allowed adversity to teach you a lesson.

6. Next time adversity occurs, accept it as a planned event for your ultimate benefit. How might this new attitude serve you?

10
Slothful Service

The blahs are inevitable when we know we're actually unneeded or unwanted or see ourselves to be so even if we aren't. God wants each of us to present ourselves for His service. He never has a surplus of dedicated workers to accomplish His task. Regardless of our profession, stature, wealth, or educational level, He can use us mightily to influence those within our realm of contact.

I've dedicated my life to Him, rededicated my life, re-rededicated my life and on it goes. There seems to be no end to my good intentions; yet if I were truly sincere one dedication would prove sufficient.

Time and time again I've told Him, "I'm ready for you to reign as undisputed Lord of my life." Shortly thereafter I declare myself ineligible for any of a variety of reasons.

Notice, the Lord doesn't say, "I can't use you" for He has promised to direct my paths and give me the needed strength if I commit my life to Him. I alone exercise my free will and option to withdraw my services and therefore denounce His Lordship.

I make the decision to go back on my word for a variety of reasons, many of which involve perceptions of myself and incorrect conclusions about the God I profess to love.

The Cop-Out

In talking to others I've discovered that many of us make our decision based upon our past. We say, "But, Lord, my past is so bad and erratic, I'm sure you can't use me." Some feel unusable because of past indiscretions while others feel, "Why make another commitment I can't keep? I've blown it every time before."

As a result of these feelings we remain tied in knots and anxiety ridden, doubting our self-worth and God's ability to use someone characterized by such imperfection.

Certainly we believe the Word of God and the fact that "He is the same yesterday, today, and forever"; yet somehow we fail to allow this professed belief to bridge the problem of our usability.

If we examine the Scriptures, clear illustrations abound that show God's ability and willingness to tap the potential of those whose past has been deeply pockmarked by sins that are considered gross even by worldly standards. Paul was a blasphemer. He hated Jesus and persecuted Christians and even watched them die. By his own admission (see 1 Tim. 1:12-17) he was a violent aggressor whose chief desire was to eradicate Christianity. Yet God showed Paul great mercy, forgave the "chief of all sinners" (have you ever killed a fellow Christian?) and then welcomed him into His services.

Knowing this, can you really believe your past renders you unusable to Paul's God?

Whenever we dwell on our past we are immobilized in the future. Our God has promised us freedom from our past, "If we confess our sins, He is faithful and righteous to forgive our sins and to cleanse us from all unrighteousness" (1 John 1:9), and since He is unchanging we are guaranteed the same "mercy" Paul speaks of in 1 Timothy 1:16.

Yes, God shows mercy for us; yet His purpose reaches beyond the level where we feel cleansed.

When He frees us from our past, we are free to serve Him

in the present, unencumbered by guilt or unworthiness. His mercy and forgiveness benefit us in order that we more effectively may serve Him.

The Misfit

Some would undoubtedly argue that Paul's past was forgiven because he committed those sins prior to his conversion experience. They support their unusableness as they rebut, "I sinned after my salvation experience so I'm no longer a fit vessel." This contention is proven false when one reads the account of Peter in Mark 14:66-72.

Peter had been personally trained by Jesus. Imagine sitting under the ministry of the Master for nearly three years. Most of us would give anything for that experience. Surely Peter would be spiritually mature and equal to any task.

Along came Peter's biggest chance to support Jesus Christ and he blew it. Not only did he blow it once, but twice, and then the third time. I don't know about you, but if I had spent three years of my life personally training an employee, only to have him blow his big chance three times, I would have told him to take a hike.

But Jesus refrained from giving Peter his walking papers. He allowed Peter to continue in His service. In fact, Mark 16:7 tells us that after Jesus rose from the dead He issued instructions to "go, tell [the] disciples and Peter" to meet Him in Galilee. Not only had Jesus forgiven Peter, but He actually personalized an invitation to Peter to meet Him at a prearranged location.

Because of the way Jesus forgave Peter and showed mercy, Peter was freed up to serve effectively. Approximately 50 days after he had denied Jesus, Peter started the Christian church at Pentecost.

Yes, not only can God forgive the past of people who sinned prior to salvation, but He is all-sufficient to forgive believers and use them mightily.

Peter and Paul are considered by many to be foundational to the Christian church; yet both of them required forgiveness and mercy for past transgressions before they could render effective service.

The Anxious

Paul encourages us to forget "what lies behind and [reach] forward to what lies ahead" (Phil. 3:13); yet to some of us the "future" poses as significant a roadblock to service as the past.

In Matthew 6:25-34, Jesus calls our attention to the futility of anxiety. Yet millions of professing Christians are so heavily laden with worry about the future, they're next to useless in the present. Jesus gives a clue to our anxieties when, in verse 33, He indicates our future will be taken care of if our priorities are in order. In effect He lets us know that seeking His kingdom first will lessen our self-centeredness, thus reducing our anxieties about the future.

Many people spend 30 percent of their time worrying about their past ("Oh how I've blown it"), and 35 percent of their time worrying about their future ("I wonder what's going to happen to me?"), leaving a meager 35 percent of their available energies with which to deal with the present. They then sit in amazement wondering why they've accomplished so little and complaining "how time flies."

How much more effective our lives would be if we would commit the past to Christ (accept His complete forgiveness), commit the future to Him (knowing He has promised to supply our every need), thus freeing 100 percent of ourselves to living in the present.

Lord, thanks for giving me the chance to serve. Help me trust in you and not be afraid of the future or guilty about the past so that I might serve you completely with the joy which comes through reasonable service.

Exercise for Understanding

1. What event in David's life would cast a doubt upon his fitness for service?

2. Have you ever been blessed by someone's ministry only later to discover, by his own admission, that he had been deeply involved in sin while ministering to you? How did you feel?

3. Is it important for people who minister to be honest about their sin and failures? Why?

4. Complete the following statement:
   I haven't kept my past commitments to serve Christ because I feared:

5. During the next month, each time you catch yourself worrying about your future, make a commitment to read Matthew 6:25-34 and Proverbs 3:5,6.

══ 11 ══
Over-Receiving

To many of us, the accumulation of material possessions represents happiness. We want the biggest home, the newest car, the latest appliances, and a fashionable wardrobe. Anything less leaves us with a case of the blahs; how can we be happy when we haven't received the best?

The materialistic urge is so strong that many of us hover on the brink of bankruptcy with a revolving account in each department store, VISA and Mastercharge cards approaching the credit limit, plus an instant credit loan or two. To work our way out of the dilemma, we fall for a "consolidation loan" to pay off all our indebtedness only to maximize it again during the next calendar year.

No wonder the hippie generation of the sixties denounced our materialistic culture while proposing an alternative existence. (It would be interesting to see if advertising has worked those hippies into our "establishment" rut by now.)

Programmed to Receive

From earliest childhood, most Americans are programmed to become receivers. Great anticipation surrounds Christmas as each little tot awaits the arrival of Santa with stacks of presents. Even though we try to stress the real meaning of Christmas, most children cannot escape without the distinct impression that "receiving" alone brings happiness. We reinforce "the joy of receiving" by loading children down with presents on their birthday; we bring outsiders into the act as we stage a full-fledged party inviting junior's playmates to the grand event. Of course, every mother is fully aware that her invited child should go to the party fully equipped with present in hand.

The birthday and Christmas child frantically fights the ribbon and tears the paper, tunneling his way through the pile of gifts. He devotes only enough time required to identify the gift before he discards it to the toy box, in many cases never to pay attention to it again.

Not wanting to chance insufficient programming, we outfit our kids in Halloween costumes and let them raid the neighborhood to see how much they can "get" since "getting" is where it's at.

Those neighbors who fail to fork over a candy bar or pack of chewing gum, regardless of the reason, become fair game because they're violating our children's "right to receive."

My purpose in reviewing our holiday patterns is not to encourage abandonment of these traditional family gatherings, for such would be tantamount to denouncing motherhood and apple pie. I do wish, however, to emphasize that most of us have been programmed since infanthood to become receivers, and I encourage parents to seek alternative methods of celebrating that will elevate the significance of each special occasion and the specialness of family, friendship, and God-given individual worth. Celebration times should de-emphasize receiving.

After such effective childhood education, is it any wonder that children throw temper tantrums at the local shopping center when parents say no to the latest advertised toy or snack food? Junior has a hard time reconciling the fact that for several years we taught him that joy comes through receiving, now we have the audacity to say no to his demands in the supermarket.

Time and time again, the guilt-laden parent succumbs to the screaming child and buys the item in question which further reinforces the receiving syndrome.

The receiver goes to school with inherent problems. Every school and classroom with which I've been associated has been plagued by a percentage of receivers who sit back, devoid of any legitimate effort, while openly declaring or stating through their actions, "I'm here, teacher, fill me with knowledge." They are also the first to gripe to the administrator in charge when they receive grades commensurate with their effort.

The receiver oriented adolescent is characterized by wanting others to provide for him. He rarely contributes to the household yet expects more than his share of the benefits. Mom can work, clean, and cook and Dad can do the same, yet Junior has to be threatened before he pitches in.

It's a rude awakening when upon entering the job market the receiver discovers that he must put forth a bonafide effort or accept his "pink slip."

But does our happiness truly depend on what we receive? Newspapers regularly carry stories about suicides among people who, by the world's standards, had all they could ever desire. Evidently accumulating things isn't really the key.

Proper Priority

In reading Scriptures, some believers feel they must either denounce all material possessions or jeopardize their salvation. God did not intend that Christians whom He has blessed with material things, should be on a perpetual guilt trip as they view their possessions. We should not read with trepidation and guilt, "Do not love the world, nor the things in the world. If any one loves the world, the love of the Father is not in him" (1 John 2:15), or, "Set your mind on the things above, not on the things that are on earth'' (Col. 3:2).

While these verses do indeed caution us not to become enamored with worldly possessions, they do not pronounce "things" as wrong. Things are neither good nor bad. It is impossible to place a qualitative value on inanimate objects. What God is telling us in these verses of Scripture is that when we become a slave to our possessions and they require an inordinate amount of our time, resources and energies, then they do become wrong for us.

As long as we keep the correct priorities before God, I fully believe He intends for Christians to have the best. When He says, "Seek first His kingdom, and His righteousness; and all these things shall be added to you" (Matt. 6:33), I've noticed no cross reference specifying "things" as "second-hand furniture" or "except microwaves and Cadillacs" or "not to exceed a $50,000 dwelling except in Southern California."

When God says through Paul, "You will be enriched in everything for all liberality" (2 Cor. 9:11), I believe He denounces Christian pauperism for those who adhere to His priorities.

Matthew 25:21 also indicates the Lord may well entrust us with additional things when He finds us faithful with the possessions He's currently blessed us with.

The Greatest Gifts

As if our earthly training wasn't sufficient to make us pedigree receivers, our heavenly Father, in great mercy, showers us with the gifts of His Son—forgiveness, strength, and eternal life. At the same time, He pronounces that all of us who accept His gift are heirs with Him and joint-heirs with Jesus Christ.

So here I sit, a perfected 40-year-old receiver, when all at once I become aware that Jesus said, "It is more blesssed to give than to receive" (Acts 20:35). I've had such little practice giving I squirm when I read, "Give, and it will be given to you; good measure, pressed down; shaken together, running over, they will pour into your lap. For whatever measure you deal out to others, it will be dealt to you in return" (Luke 6:38).

Our preoccupation with money and materialism causes us to believe that the "giving" Jesus talks about must be financially oriented; in reality the giving may include our time, our resources, our talents, our love.

Eva was passing through deep waters. She was only 17 years old and her mom had recently succumbed to a two-year bout with cancer. Not being a gifted student, Eva could hardly cope with her schoolwork, much less cook, wash clothes, keep house and mother her four younger brothers and sisters. The strain was so great that Eva contemplated suicide on several occasions.

Connie, a high school friend, was led of the Lord to take an interest in Eva's plight. She saw Eva several times a week, picked her up for youth meetings, took her out to eat, phoned her daily to let Eva know she cared.

Although Eva still feels pressured and burdened concerning her future, she thanks Connie every time they're together for being such a help and encouragement.

Connie's service involved very little financially, but she gave a wealth of love, warmth, and concern.

Giving in reality cannot be separated from service and our Lord places a premium on service. He considered it so significant that while passing through the darkest hour of His life, with the cross hanging over His head, He took time to show the full extent of His love (see John 13:1). He girded Himself with a towel and washed His disciples' feet as a servant would. Then He entreated them to serve each other and all mankind.

Next time you feel pressure and assume you have the right to be absorbed in your own situation, reflect on Jesus Christ who, about to be brutally killed, thought about serving others.

Interestingly, when we care for others and render service to them our problems seem fewer and less intense; for then our energies are devoted to constructively assisting others instead of dwelling on our personal concerns to such an extent that we amplify their importance. This, in the vernacular, is really "getting it together."

Jesus had it together. John 13:3,4, indicate that He knew who He was, knew His power and knew where He was going (the cross); and yet He still took time to give to others.

Unfortunately, many of us who claim to be Christians still view ourselves as receivers. We feel we have received for-giveness, received eternal life, received God's blessings; therefore we elevate ourselves above others. We stand on a pedestal looking down.

Unless we let the Holy Spirit, through God's Word, reprogram us from our status of confirmed receiver to a giver or server, our happiness will always be contingent upon our *receiving* what we believe we need. Serving is a practical demonstration of love, and giving oneself is love's highest form, as God clearly showed by giving His Son.

Serving allows us to bless others and God, thus producing joy in our lives. We alone hold the key to the degree of joy we desire; for it will be proportional to the amount we give to others in love and service.

Lord, I have truly been conditioned to receive. I need your wisdom and strength to transform me into a willing giver. Help me recognize that your example of giving was in serving others. May I through service to you and others demonstrate your love and experience the joy you intended me to have.

Thank you for the joy I know will be mine when service becomes a way of life.

Exercise for Understanding

1. What steps have you taken within your home to de-emphasize the importance of receiving?

2. Complete the following:
   I personally demonstrate service by:

3. When a person renders a service to me, my feelings towards that person are:

4. Who, excluding God, best exemplified the joy of giving during your childhood years?

5. Discuss the risks involved (if any) in service.

12
Anti-Body Christianity

We fret over selecting the right clothes, comb our hair over our bald spots, run for our cardiovascular fitness, do push-ups for our upper body, sit-ups to flatten our stomachs, diet to make the pounds fall off. We hold our breath while strutting in front of the full-length mirror, submit to face lifts, nose jobs, facial sandings, tummy tucks and breast augmentations because not many people feel good about their bodies.

The media focus on the young, the sleek, the beautiful, the sexy, and the handsome to peddle their wares. The greatest demand for products is created by duping the public into believing youth, vitality, good looks and sex appeal are attainable upon purchase and application of the product advertised.

Scantly-clad bodies, leaving little to the imagination, grace our billboards, stimulate our desires and excite sexual urges.

Unless our body conforms to the young and beautiful ones which dominate the airwaves, movie screens, and periodicals, we feel unworthy and develop the blahs. In some cases we have downright contempt for our own bodies. Disenchantment with our bodies is primarily responsible for the annual expenditure of billions of dollars for exercise gadgets, diet gimmicks, cosmetic surgeries, and spa and exercise salon memberships.

This close association of the body with negative societal purposes causes many Christians to ashamedly mentally disassociate themselves from their bodies.

Christ Wants Your Body

We anti-body Christians enter a state of conflict when we read, ''I urge you therefore, brethren, by the mercies of God, to present your bodies a living and holy sacrifice, acceptable to God, which is your spiritual service of worship'' (Rom. 12:1).

Certainly, God can't literally want this body of mine? So we search all translations of the Bible trying to clarify this obvious misunderstanding. Yet regardless of our search the fact remains: God wants my body as imperfect and tired as it is. He goes so far as to say that giving Him my body is an act of worship and is pleasing to Him.

It's finally becoming clear, as I read the Gospels, what Paul was saying to the Romans. Jesus accomplished His work on earth and His Father's purpose through His body. With His *feet* He walked to people in need; with His *hands* He reached out in healing; with His *vocal chords* He declared His purpose; with his *eyes* He showed love; with his *heart* He felt compassion. Ultimately He gave His whole body to redeem us unto Himself that through a simple act of belief we could spend eternity with Him. Hallelujah!

Yet for so long, I and many other Christians have spiritualized Christianity to the place where we saw no heavenly use for our earthly bodies. I pray that God will constantly remind me that, although a spiritual dimension is added to my life when I accept Him, He can carry on His earthly work only through our bodies.

Giving my body to Christ is as spiritual as giving my spirit to Him. The act of committing my body to His service adds dignity to my anatomy, for no higher purpose exists than that of being used for Christ's service. How can I truly give my spirit to God without my body when my spirit is housed in my body? Giving my spirit to Christ without my body is as incongruous as saying marriage vows then withholding my body from my marriage partner.

Thank God that in former times, present times, and future times we are allowed to present our bodies to Him. If the act is done in an attitude and service of love our potential, regardless of our condition, is unlimited.

"Do you not know that you are a temple of God and that the Spirit of God dwells in you? If any man destroys the temple of God, God will destroy him, for the temple of God is holy, and that is what you are" (1 Cor. 3:16,17). What an amazing truth! Each believer has, dwelling within his body, the Spirit of God.

God is pleased to accept our bodies. The act of giving them to Him constitutes worship. Worship is not confined to being in church, as important as this is, but consists of giving myself spiritually and *physically* for His service. If we see our present activity, whether play, work, or conversation, as dedicated to His service, He deems it *worship* and it brings glory to Him. As long as a body has life and breath it can lead a soul to Christ or facilitate His purposes.

Physical Imperfection Is OK

God does not say that He will use only the perfect, unblemished body. He accepted only the perfect, unblemished lamb for sacrifice, but only Jesus fulfilled that requirement among mankind. God will use any Christian's body that is committed to Him.

If broken or tired bodies were precluded from His service, every person not in optimum health would be excluded, greatly diminishing His service force and therefore the potential for good.

People like Judy Collins, who suffered congenital heart disease and succumbed a few years ago while in her senior year of high school, would not have been allowed to serve. Yet with her fragile body, Judy impacted hundreds of students with the message of Jesus Christ.

If the crippled were not allowed to serve, Joni Erickson, the quadriplegic who has used her artistry and life story to lead many people to a saving knowledge of Jesus Christ, would have been stricken from the service rolls.

In times of old, the apostle Paul, because of the thorn in his flesh which many scholars interpret as being a physical impairment, would have been declared unfit for the Master's service. God can be greatly glorified in broken bodies.

Temple Maintenance

Some accept God's desire for Christian bodies as a license for physical neglect and abuse. God does not specify that only trim, fit, healthy bodies should be given for His service and all those out-of-shape physiques should be discarded to the junk heap. But He does assign His Holy Spirit to dwell within us and declares our bodies to be His temple. So it befits us to preserve and maintain this temple.

When we're expecting company to visit our homes, most of us practically turn our houses upside down in the hopes of impressing our visitors.

In contrast, many of us defile our bodies to such an extent through overeating or other abuse that I wonder if the Spirit of God thinks He dwells in a temple or a dilapidated shack.

Yet a Christian who is sincere and desirous of pleasing God by genuine worship will not use the fact that "God wants his body" as a free ticket for letting his body dissipate, but should instead have a new mind set reflecting the following.

My body is a temple of my God. He lives within

my body, therefore by keeping my body healthy (which includes weight control), I am honoring my God by giving Him the best possible temple to live in.

If my weight is controlled and I am healthier, I'll live longer, which gives me more time on earth to serve my Master.

If I am successful in setting an example of restraint in my diet, others will ask me how I succeed and I'll witness that my God assisted me. My witness may result in a convert to my beliefs. [1]

While it is important to maintain a healthy and fit body, it is just as dangerous to overemphasize the importance of maintaining a perfect body. A healthy balance is necessary, since preoccupation with one's body can cause one to devote an inordinate amount of time and effort to caring for it to the demise of service for Christ.

Taking care of your body without going to extremes demonstrates a healthy self-concept. If you have a poor self-concept, it is hard to represent Christ effectively since it is evident that you must doubt that even His presence in your life makes you worthy, or acceptable.

Mind Renewal

"And do not be conformed to this world, but be transformed by the renewing of your mind, that you may prove what the will of God is, that which is good and acceptable and perfect" (Rom. 12:2).

This renewed mind-set should cause us to control our caloric intake and participate in regular exercise so our body can render the most effective service to Him.

"Renewing of your mind" begins with the recognition that "no way in and of myself can I please God because of my sin." This knowledge then progresses to, "I can please God now that I've received Him.'' Knowing that the Holy Spirit lives within me and allows me to do His will now provides the vehicle to merge my belief with my action as I give my life, my spirit, and my body to Him.

The cycle is now complete. Only after we trust God and believe His promises do we feel good about our bodies. Becoming a Christian does not mean ''personality annihilation'' nor does it mean I must put down any part of myself in an effort to achieve humility (false or real) to be used by God.

Lord, thanks for showing me that the most ''reasonable'' thing I can do is to recognize my body as a gift from God, and give it back to you for your service. When I've done this, I know great joy will come to you and a new level of fulfillment will come to me.

Exercise for Understanding

1. In your opinion, are most people in our society pleased with who they are or what they are? Why, or why not?

2. What fears do you have about giving yourself and your body to God?

3. What, about your body, do you feel might not be pleasing to God?

4. List some services you could render for Christ if you were willing to give your body to Him.

5. Many of us have given our bodies to Christ at one time or another only to take them back from Him. What are some of the reasons we often choose to renege on our previous commitment?

Note

1. John Dobbert, *The Love Diet* (Old Tappan, NJ: Fleming H. Revell Co., 1977), p. 57.

══ 13 ══
Over-Commitment

As a principal of a secondary school, I often fall into the trap of asking the most cooperative staff member to serve when I need someone to do something important for the school. Why? Because it's expedient. I know he'll say yes and that quick confirmation lends itself well to the most effective use of my time.

I also impose upon the one most likely to say yes because I enjoy the reinforcement of the pleasantly spoken yes as opposed to the discomfort of the, "No, I don't think I have time" routine. That negative tends to involve me emotionally and produces in me a feeling of partial rejection of me and my program. I'm sure it is similar to what a door-to-door salesman must feel when his shoe, wedged in the door, is the only salvation to his nose being flattened.

I immensely resent the obvious misuse of people for the benefit of others or the institution they represent.

When a public figure professes his new-found faith in Christ, he is often hustled to the media by the evangelical opportunists in much the same manner as a new product dominates the television screen prior to the holiday season. One would think the conversion of this public figure somehow brought final credibility to our faith.

Once he makes his profession, the new believer will be hurled from talk show to talk show, and from crusade to seminar, whether or not he is mature enough spiritually to withstand the onslaught of questions. His eagerness to serve and cooperate can easily wane to resentment as he begins to sense that he is being exploited as a commodity. This resentment increases if he is unable to invest sufficient time to produce effectively in his chosen profession.

I wonder how many public figures avoid exposure to the gospel because they know what the Christian world would demand of them if their commitment were discovered. I also wonder how many do not publicly profess their salvation for the same reason.

Certainly one should be eager to share his new-found faith which could lead to numerous people making a like commitment. But a new Christian needs sufficient time and opportunity to read and study God's Word, leading to a more mature and deeper faith.

This misuse is certainly not limited to public figures for many churches participate in the abuse of the committed.

I have great compassion for the pastor who falls into the trap of further committing the over-committed with unsuspecting ease. If it's difficult to find someone to serve on a committee or supervise an activity in an organization where future advancement in salary could be affected, how much more difficult it must be to get people to commit themselves when their only motivation is love.

The pastor soon, consciously or subconsciously, identifies the ''low risk, least likely to say no'' group. And each need which becomes evident in the fellowship finds him gravitating to its members.

After all, he wants to feel good, too, and their willingness reinforces his feeling that his time and effort are being rewarded, since his message is obviously getting through. In addition, if anyone needs to use his time wisely, a pastor does. Those visits to the sick, the decisions regarding finances, the replacement of the youth pastor who has just resigned, the counseling session with that family about to break up, that small group of people who seems overly excited about the Holy Spirit, those six families who didn't like last Sunday's background music—all consume enormous amounts of time.

So, because of their willingness to get involved and their inability to say no, the committed few are soon involved in every activity the church supports.

The Plight of the Over-Involved

Some may question, What's wrong with that? Shouldn't those who love their Lord be involved? After all, Paul stated, "I urge you therefore, brethren, by the mercies of God, to present your bodies a living and holy sacrifice, acceptable to God, which is your spiritual service of worship" (Rom. 12:1).

There's nothing wrong with commitment; in fact, 2 Corinthians 8:7,8 indicates that your willingness to serve proves the earnestness and sincerity of your love. Verse 5 of the same chapter indicates that stewardship begins with giving ourselves. But there's plenty wrong with over-commitment. And unless your church is unusual, there's a nucleus of over-committed and over-taxed people within your Body.

Larry served as sales representative for several prominent lines of furniture. His warm, easygoing manner contributed much to his sales success and placed him in contention for the position of national sales manager for a large furniture manufacturer.

Throughout the industry and within his community and church Larry was known as a people person, for all who knew him, liked him.

When he entered First Community Church, Larry and his

potential were immediately noticed by the staff. Soon requests to serve seemed to come on a weekly basis.

Larry at first was flattered. He graciously accepted the position of high school Sunday School teacher and his involvement and the appreciation expressed provided a feeling of belonging.

As resignations occurred and positions remained unfilled, Larry soon inherited the midweek college and career class and, each month, he rotated as the teacher for the adults. What began as a welcome responsibility soon became drudgery as responsibilities and hours doubled and tripled.

Insensitive to the overload, the staff asked more and more of Larry until his expanded jobs included chairman of the deacon board and director of the Christian Endeavor movement.

Maybe Larry's inability to say no was a result of the training of his father, a minister. But in his own words Larry stated, "Saying no to the pastor seemed wrong and I knew I would have felt awfully guilty if I had."

Then, one day the pastor left and guess who became chairman of the pulpit committee?

Larry left the church soon after the new pastor came aboard. He sought a new church where he could worship with some anonymity without being deluged with requests to serve. But within a short time, Larry was again discovered, over-involved, and the joy of service turned to the drudgery of over-extension.

In a recent conversation with Larry, I was surprised to discover he hasn't been a part of any church for more than four years.

"We stay at home and watch church services on television and I feel my faith is as strong as ever. I do miss the fellowship, but I no longer have to spend most of my waking hours in church-related activities while resenting those who criticize yet fail to carry their share of the load."

From Joy to Resentment

When people consent to over-involvement, invariably their attitude changes from one of joyous service to one of resentment as the rigorous schedule takes a toll on their physical and mental well-being. When resentful attitudes result, it keeps the well-meaning, committed people from the blessings usually derived through joyful service.

Secularly we discuss "the law of diminishing returns," yet somehow we expect the spiritual facet of our lives to be exempt from such entrapments. This "law" does, however, apply to all areas of our life. Often a person functions effectively when he serves in one or two areas of church ministry, yet when asked to serve in additional facets of the program he does nothing well. Because he is spread over too many fronts, the effort necessary to operate effectively is dissipated and results in frustration.

We are entreated to "do all unto the glory of God" yet this becomes nearly impossible when our hearts and minds are filled with resentment due to over-extension.

Over-extension also may reap havoc with relationships within the Body as the members carrying the lion's share of the responsibilities begin to resent others in the Body who they perceive as not doing their job. Obviously, the fulfilling fellowship these people once enjoyed suffers immeasurably, thus negatively affecting the entire Body.

Statements such as, "They take and take but never give of themselves," and, "I am involved in everything plus work 40 hours a week and they're not employed at all but still don't help," are signs of discontent among those who are overworked.

Those assuming more than their share of responsibilities within the Body would be alarmed to know that they are performing a disservice to others within the fellowship. As they continue to say yes and accept additional responsibilities, regardless of the negative effects, others are deprived of service and the resulting fulfillment. Their growth and maturity are therefore limited.

Some, who never have had the chance, desire to serve and finally leave the fellowship when their offers are refused. They were probably rejected for service because they lacked maturity, yet how can they develop unless they are used? Who should be more tolerant than the Body of Christ?

This denial of an opportunity to serve is likened to the person seeking employment who is continually rejected due to lack of experience. When will he ever be allowed to gain some experience that will result in growth?

I submit that pastors are often guilty of affecting the total fellowship by taking the path of least resistance when they continue to bombard the soft-touch for the sure yes.

Just as pastors should be sensitive to the limit of service one can assume effectively, we, as lay people, must also be honest and open with our pastors concerning how we perceive our limitations.

The Danger of Overextending

For the benefit of the entire Body, pastors should reach out to others and solicit their involvement, even at the risk of receiving a no. Some pastors cannot accept a no without personalizing it to mean, "I don't support you or your ministry." But God will give the pastor the ability to accept negative responses and the reasons for them.

Don't always choose the soft touch. Reach out. Jesus called people in all walks of life. He called a tax collector as well as a rough, impetuous fisherman to serve Him. Should you avoid that corporate executive, that hod carrier, or the owner of the local bakery? Some are teetering on the brink and need only be asked to serve in some capacity commensurate with their spiritual maturity and talent. When the Holy Spirit prepares a heart for service, He pays no heed to sex, age, or profession.

The over-involved member often risks deterioration of his God-given priorities. God doesn't expect us to compromise our convictions and priorities in order to serve Him. If we are involved to the extent that our best use of time does not allow us to meet the needs of our family or perform to our usually high standards within our job, our service is not pleasing to Him who has told us to do *all* unto the glory of God.

It is as important for pastors to advise people to reduce the scope of their Christian service, when it's obvious their family and other priorities are suffering, as it is to encourage them to become committed. Often the child of a committed-to-Christ, over-indulged Christian has viewed his frustrated, anxiety-ridden, no-fun Dad or Mom and outwardly or inwardly voiced, "I want none of it," as he forever turns his back on any element of Christian service.

Although some pastors adhere to the belief that "ambitious people derive slight joy, if any, when their ability remains uncontested,"[1] contesting often is confused with deluging. I seriously doubt whether God will bless others through our ministry when our home and family have figuratively gone to hell as a result of over-serving.

I believe that over-serving, at the expense of our family's welfare, is sin. What fulfillment and blessing can you derive from service when your family unit is coming apart at the seams?

Over-extension in many cases prevents one from being spiritually fed. No time to be fed yet having to feed others is a real danger. For a limited time we can survive but over a lengthy duration this diet will result in spiritual malnutrition. We must receive if we are to give and minister effectively to others. And unless we first open our fists and let go of excessive responsiblities, God cannot refill our hands and hearts. If over-extension continually interferes with ingestion of spiritual truths and lessons, we are the losers.

Limiting the Growth of the Body

When a select group takes on too many functions of the church, the entire Body is prevented from growing (not only spiritually but in number as well).

Fifty percent of the churches today have a regular average attendance of less than 75 people in their fellowship. Eighty percent of the churches in America have a regular attendance of less than 200 people. Ninety-five percent of the churches have an average attendance of between 200 and 350 people and only 5 percent of the churches in America today have an average attendance of over 350 people.[2]

One of the reasons for these small attendances could well be that when we overburden the few within the fellowship, and neglect to seek and recruit others to serve, there aren't enough people to provide the personal attention to those who visit the fellowship to confirm that they indeed are important as individuals and are vital to this Body of believers.

Without the discipling of additional members within the fellowship, both those who come regularly and those who visit periodically will be left unattended. When this is the case, don't be surprised when members become conspicuously absent week after week and soon fade from the fellowship completely.

As the church grows in number, the church staff usually grows to keep pace with the demands of the ministry. Every bit as important as added staff is the continual discipling of willing helpers to meet the personal needs of the Body members.

Why People Overextend

If overextension produces such negative results, why then does it occur with such regularity? There are several reasons:

We feel guilty when we say no. Saying no to our pastor is likened to saying no to God and how can we say no to Him who gave His all for us? This may be a rude awakening, but saying yes to avoid guilt is not a worthy motivation for Christian service.

We must learn to say no when saying yes would increase our level of service to the extent that we would abandon the priorities God has given us.

Saying no doesn't lessen our commitment to our Saviour. We can still be highly committed but realize our limitations and remember our obligations to fulfill the responsibilities to our family, job, friends, and other Christians. We must be honest and not allow ourselves to be pushed beyond our ability to serve effectively while maintaining our priorities.

Furthermore, saying yes when our heart is saying no is dishonest and God will not bless a dishonest or resentful servant. If you serve with this attitude, you rob yourself of blessing.

We worry about our Christian image. What will the pastor think when I say no? What will other people think? I suggest that you explain your reasons fully and then worship without concern about your image. As long as you're honest in your heart, your credibility with God is secure. After all, if we are serving to receive the respect and plaudits of men instead of a desire to please God, we have already received our reward.

If we don't take that extra job, the program may fail. At times the greatest lessons are learned by allowing failure. If we over-protect our child from failure by doing his homework each time he says, "I don't understand," soon he has us sufficiently trained, and we suffer along with an additional burden as he romps off scot-free.

This illustration has spiritual application as well. If we continue to throw ourselves over the hole in the dam to prevent failure of programs, others will fail to get involved. When the program looks as if it might fail or falter, however, volunteers often come forward to shoulder the responsibility.

Some seek immersion in church programs to avoid deal-

ing with unpleasant situations. Those who are in charge of enlisting helpers in the church must be aware that some people volunteer for every announced need. While we may marvel at this degree of commitment, it soon becomes apparent that keeping busy in the church is providing a means to avoid an unpleasant home or personal situation.

If this is the case, the pastor must limit the service and encourage efforts towards resolving the problems.

Limiting Your Commitment

How do you know when you are serving God at your optimum? (1) When you feel slightly taxed yet fulfilled in service, but you can still effectively devote time to your other responsibilities—family, home, job. (2) When God is blessing your ministry with fruit. (3) When you are stimulated to recreate. (4) When you are still being fed from the Word of God and have fellowship with other believers.

How do you know when you have surpassed your level of most effective service? (1) Resentment begins creeping into your attitude. (2) You're consistently tired. (3) Your other obligations are suffering. (4) You don't look forward to serving. (5) Other people comment about your lack of enthusiasm. (6) When you can't see fruit for your labor. (7) When you don't have time to study God's Word in your own devotion time.

I know of no more fulfilling experience than serving Christ effectively. I unequivocably recommend it to all believers. There is joy in serving Jesus.

The successful churches use, not abuse, their members wisely. They are sensitive to the outside pressures faced by those serving Christ; they encourage open and honest feedback from those involved; they focus considerable efforts in discipling others to share in the ministry; they are sensitive to the needs of the willing and insist periodically that they take a break from service; they provide quality training to increase the skills of those who serve; they offer a choice of service when someone appears to be "just the right person" for another responsibility; they fully accept a no or lessening of service as the need arises without laying on a guilt trip, questioning one's spirituality or coercing by threatening to eliminate a program.

I trust you will experience the joy and fulfillment which comes through *effective* service and pray that those responsible for recruitment of servers will be sensitive to that group of committed believers who get in over their head and thereby lessen their personal effectiveness and productivity and that of the Body of Christ.

Lord, keep me keenly aware of all my responsibilities and from this day forward, may I seek a balance which would be healthy for me and those I love, and glorifying to you.

Exercise for Understanding
1. Do you feel a relationship exists between the number of jobs you perform in the church and the effectiveness with which they're accomplished?

2. Could you say no to a request by your pastor to assist in a new church program? Describe how you would respond to this request.

3. In all *honesty*, describe some of the reasons you've served the Lord in the past.

Discuss with someone else whether the reasons you listed are constructive reasons for serving.

4. Describe at least three attributes which characterize a person who in your estimation serves well in your church.

Notes

1. Bruce C. Ogilvie, "Psychological Consistencies," *Journal of the American Medical Association*, 1968, pp. 205, 780-786.
2. C. Peter Wagner, *American Church Growth* (Wheaton, IL: National Association of Evangelicals, 1974).

14

Yo-Yo Christianity

My Christian life has been characterized by peaks and valleys, surges and stagnancy.

From my earliest Christian experiences, "It was high in July" and a "bust in August." The July summer camp experience, rich with Christian fun, fellowship and instruction in the Word of God, provided me with intense excitement and real joy I just knew was going to last.

One week later the joy faded and the excitement was diluted by the demanding mundane responsibilities of everyday living. The excitement of that first job, my new driver's license, the basketball season, and the discovery that girls were more than boys with long hair, made it pretty difficult for Christianity to compete for supremacy in my life.

Yo-Yo Christianity would have been an apropos term to characterize my faith.

"Up on Sunday, down on Monday" was a pattern oft repeated during my teen years.

"Certainly stability will enter my Christian walk when I become an adult," I often reasoned.

Now, with 20 years of adulthood behind me, my faith to some may still appear to be of the elevator variety.

The couples conference constitutes a mountaintop experience which strengthens my faith and causes me to view in

proper perspective my daily experiences. But, having re-
turned home to be greeted by a business deal gone awry, or
confronted by a problem involving my teenage daughter, my
faith bubble bursts and I abruptly hit rock bottom.

Is that the way my faith is designed to be? Should my
Christianity only excite me when I sit under the ministry of
Billy Graham or another of God's choice servants, take part
in a deeper-life conference, or spend a working week under
the tutelage of Bill Gothard? Does my faith come in massive
doses at infrequent intervals, or can my faith become an
exciting day-to-day living experience through regular planned nurturing without the necessity of a "super experience"
away from the rigors of everyday life?

I live in an area which, before development, consisted
almost entirely of citrus orchards. Driving past the orchards, I
often observed large ditches being dug at the drip line along
each row of trees. After the digging was completed, the water
was turned on to flood the ditches to capacity. When the water
neared the top of the ditches it was abruptly shut off in time to
allow slow absorption into the tree roots before the surplus
water exceeded the banks and spilled over into non-planted
areas.

This process was repeated over and over again at pre-
determined intervals. Even though great care was exercised
to insure frugal use of the water supply, there always was a
broken bank here, water exceeding its banks there, or water
rushing through a newly-dug gopher hole, defeating the
purpose of the system. If the ditch was not readily repaired,
those trees not getting water soon showed the effects of
drought. But the flooded area reaped an unwanted harvest of
unruly weeds.

Then, a few years ago, watering practices changed.
Thousands of feet of flexible hose were systematically wound
through the orchard to encircle each tree. No ditches, no
surging water, no weeds; the trees look greener, healthier,

and more heavily laden with fruit than ever before. Ranchers claim the new system saves water, decreases bothersome weeds, greatly reduces water bills and increases efficiency and production.

Upon close examination of the system, I observed the "emitters" which had been interjected into the hose at equal intervals surrounding each tree. Lifting a portion of the hose off the ground I saw the steady drip, drip, drip, drip of water drops. Even when the system had been operating for 24 hours, only a small wet spot (a few inches in diameter) was under each emitter. Yet below the surface the saturated area fans out like a triangle to include a vast number of root ends.

Having observed the results of both systems, the evidence clearly supported abandoning the old in favor of adopting the new. The benefits of the orchard drip system to the fruit grower are increased growth, deeper and better established roots (stronger growing), less waste, greater efficiency, increased stability and more abundant fruit.

If we as Christians, day by day as regularly as the drip system, infuse Christ into our lives, the benefits will be exactly the same. The process of infusion involves a *steady* diet of reading God's Word, prayer, and fellowshipping with other believers.

Note the word steady. Steady connotes regularity. The sporadic practice of Scripture reading, prayer and fellowship, while certain to benefit somewhat, will not produce the consistent growth we need in order to be fulfilled.

Abide in Christ

One can be a Christian without abiding in Christ but not without Him abiding in you. "Abiding" is entirely different from being associated with, for it entails being obedient to God and His Word; and to do this you must spend time with Him.

Jesus said, "Abide in Me, and I in you. As the branch

cannot bear fruit of itself, unless it abides in the vine, so neither can you, unless you abide in Me'' (John 15:4).

''Abiding'' is a full-time, day to day experience which is not conditional upon external circumstances. If we truly abide, we don't turn our back on Christ Monday, Wednesday and Friday while abiding in Him on Tuesday, Thursday, and Sunday.

Paul prays that ''Christ may dwell in your hearts through faith; and that you, being rooted and grounded in love, may be able to comprehend with all the saints what is the breadth and length and height and depth, and to know the love of Christ which surpasses knowledge, that you may be filled up to all the fulness of God'' (Eph. 3:17-19).

Several times Scriptures refer to being rooted in Christ, or rooted in love. With our roots firmly planted in Him we can tap His strength and power to add stability and fulfillment to our lives.

''For even though I am absent in body, nevertheless I am with you in spirit, rejoicing to see your good discipline and the *stability* of your faith in Christ. As you therefore have received Christ Jesus the Lord, so walk in Him, having been firmly rooted and now being built up in Him and established in your faith, just as you were instructed, and overflowing with gratitude'' (Col. 2:5,6,7).

When we are grounded in Christ, His Spirit is in us and when our mind is controlled by the Spirit we have life and peace (see Rom. 8:6).

The benefits of the orchard drip system to the fruit grower are increased growth, deeper and better established roots, less waste, greater efficiency, increased stability and more abundant fruit.

Study God's Word

Without knowing the Word of God it is impossible to abide in Him. Abiding requires obedience to His Word and we must study it to know His plan for our life. "Faith comes from hearing, and hearing by the Word of Christ" (Rom. 10:17). "Grow in the grace and *knowledge* of our Lord and Savior Jesus Christ" (2 Pet. 3:18). "Thy *word* I have treasured in my heart, that I may not sin against Thee" (Ps. 119:11). "Let the *word* of Christ richly dwell within you" (Col. 3:16). "All Scripture is inspired by God and profitable for teaching, for reproof, for correction, for training in righteousness" (2 Tim. 3:16).

A regular diet of reading and memorizing God's Word while being sensitive to His Holy Spirit will greatly enhance your chances of growth towards maturity. (In fact, they are prerequisites.)

Communicate Through Prayer

While God uses His Word as the vehicle through which He communicates to us, we communicate with Him through prayer.

We're told: to "*pray* without ceasing" (1 Thess. 5:17); "Devote yourselves to *prayer,* keeping alert in it with an attitude of thanksgiving" (Col. 4:2).

"Be anxious for nothing, but in everything by *prayer* and supplication with thanksgiving let your requests be made known to God. And the peace of God, which surpasses all comprehension, shall guard your hearts and your minds in Christ Jesus" (Phil. 4:6,7).

"If you want to know what God wants you to do, *ask* him, and he will gladly tell you, for he is always ready to give a bountiful supply of wisdom to all who ask him; he will not resent it" (Jas. 1:5, *TLB*).

"And in the same way the Spirit also helps our weakness; for we do not know how to pray as we should, but the Spirit Himself intercedes for us with groanings too deep for words" (Rom. 8:26).

What a beautiful privilege. We can have instant access

into His presence through prayer and don't even have to be a professional "pray-er," for when we feel unable to pray properly His Spirit does so for us.

Fellowship with Others

If we abide in Christ, the desire to fellowship with others, serve others and minister to their needs, will be a natural outgrowth, for God's Word says: "And let our people also learn to engage in good deeds to meet pressing needs, that they may not be unfruitful" (Titus 3:14); "And do not neglect doing good and sharing; for with such sacrifices God is pleased" (Heb. 13:16); "And let us consider how to stimulate one another to love and good deeds, not forsaking our own assembling together, as is the habit of some, but encouraging one another; and all the more as you see the day drawing near" (Heb. 10:24,25).

Without sharing fellowship with other believers you are disobeying God and your faith lacks the total perspective God intended it to have. Inbreeding, without reaching out to minister to others, or allowing others to minister to you, precludes growth towards Christian maturity.

Many people seem incapable of viewing Jesus Christ except through the lives of other people. Sharing your life with them opens the door for Jesus Christ to minister to their spirit.

Regular Bible reading, a consistent prayer life, and Christian fellowship are necessary ingredients for spiritual growth.

Process of Growth

The process of growth begins the moment we invite Christ into our life, continues throughout our earthly pilgrimage and consummates when we join Him in eternity.

"But speaking the truth in love, we are to grow up in all aspects into Him, who is the head, even Christ" (Eph. 4:15); "The Spirit Himself bears witness with our spirit that we are children of God, and if children, heirs also, heirs of God and fellow-heirs with Christ'' (Rom. 8:16,17).

''Beloved, now we are children of God, and it has not appeared as yet what we shall be. We know that, if He should appear, *we shall be like Him*, because we shall see Him just as He is'' (1 John 3:2, italics added). Our growth will reach its optimum only when we in eternity become like Him.

Shall we then discontinue our efforts aimed at growth while awaiting that time? Absolutely not. If we are to obey Christ (which brings power), be freed up, and experience ever increasing levels of fulfillment, in and through Him, *we must grow*.

Most would readily concur that physical growth would be impossible without eating, breathing and exercise. Spiritual growth is likewise impossible without eating (ingesting God's Word), breathing (talking to God in prayer), and exercise (fellowshipping with others and sharing Christ) on a regular basis. This recipe should constitute the diet for any sincere Christian who desires to become more Christlike.

As we progress towards maturity through our steady involvement with Christ, the by-products will be many, not the least of which will be increased fruit for Christ and His Kingdom.

My goal should not be to bring others to Jesus, but to lift Jesus up knowing that He will draw all men unto Himself (see John 12:32).

I can lift Him up and make Him visible through my life, my attitude of service, my verbal witness and the love I demonstrate for others.

I've become convinced that I'll never be able to exist every minute on a mountaintop. But with a steady infusion of God's Word into my life, a consistent communication network between Him and me, and frequent periods of fellowship with other believers sharing love, joys, sorrows, victories and defeats in situations similar to mine, a stability and contentment will be added to my life which will lessen the extent to which I can be manipulated by my environment.

Spiritual Shock Absorber

While God wants me to live a victorious life I've found no one in the recorded Scripture or here on earth who hasn't experienced the highs and lows or the joys and disappointments which characterize my life.

The victorious Christian, however, differs from the average man or stagnant Christian in the manner in which he faces these situations. Having claimed Jesus as Lord, he views all that enters his life, whether negative or positive, as being allowed by Jesus Christ for the purpose of producing growth and ultimately bringing glory to Christ.

Highs and lows will always exist as long as we're subject to the human ebb and flow; but the mind-set with which we view them will determine whether we succumb to a lengthy residency in the pits or avert them by accepting the stability Christ offers through His Holy Spirit's presence in our life.

My constant recognition that His Holy Spirit is residing in me and has allowed today's circumstances, levels out the lows and highs of life. At the risk of not attributing the appropriate honor to the Holy Spirit, He acts as a shock absorber in cushioning life's blows while stabilizing us in high times by reminding us of our dependence on Him.

The song entitled ''Mountain Top'' so ably capsulizes the truths we've discussed.

I love to sing and I love to pray,
Worship the Lord most everyday.
I go to the temple, and I want to stay
To hide away from the hustle of the world
    and its ways.

And I'd love to live on a mountain top
Fellowshipping with the Lord,
I'd love to stand on a mountain top
'Cause I love to feel my spirit soar.
But I've got to come down from that mountain top
To the people in the valley below,
Or they'll never know that they can go

To the mountain of the Lord.
Now, praising the Father is a good thing to do.
Worship the Trinity in spirit and truth,
But if we worshipped all of the time
There would be no one to lead the blind.

Now, I am not saying that worship is wrong,
But worship is more than just singing a song.
It's all that you say, and everything that you do.
It's letting His Spirit live through you.[1]

*Lord, let me regularly commune with you through your
Word, prayer and fellowship with my brothers and sisters in
order that your enabling Spirit will allow my highs and lows
to be met with such stability that others through my life will be
drawn to you.*

Exercise for Understanding
1. Describe a time when reading the Word of God was
   instrumental in allowing you to handle more effectively a
   trying situation.

2. Can you recall a situation in the Bible in which memoriza-
   tion of the Word of God was responsible for victory over
   temptation?

3. When has a verse committed to memory aided you in recent months? Describe the situation and how the verse was applicable.

4. What evidence do you possess which supports the belief that God answers prayer?

5. Is fellowship with other believers really vital, or is its importance overstated?

   What are the benefits derived through fellowship?

Note

1. "Mountain Top" by Brown Bannister. © Copyright 1977 by Bug and Bear Music, ASCAP. All rights reserved. Used by permission. Print rights administered by Word Music, Inc.

15
Spiritual Hypochondria

As I read the Word of God, I am constantly amazed at the intellect of Jesus as He conducted His earthly ministry. The questions He asked, the problems He related, and the acts He performed befuddled the wisest men of His day and attested to the fact that He indeed was divine or had a pipeline to the divine.

Then I discovered the fifth chapter of John and wondered why Jesus suddenly departed from His keen intellect and asked such an obviously absurd question.

A man who had been sick for 38 years was lying by the pool of Bethesda hoping to be first to enter the pool and be healed after the angel of the Lord stirred the waters.

When Jesus saw the infirmed man lying by the pool He asked, "Do you wish to get well?"

When I first read that question I was disappointed for I had hoped the One in whom my faith was based was more observant and astute than to ask so obvious a question. If he didn't want to get healed why would the sick man go to the trouble of having friends carry him to the poolside? Of course he wanted to get healed.

Yet the more I see of life, the more I realize the profoundness of what seemed to be so simple a question.

Jesus asks each of us that same question today, "Do you want to be healed?"

Often we, like the sick man, avoid a direct answer as we consider the benefits derived through not being whole. While being infirmed involves degrees of frustrations, pain, and heartache it also renders one free from certain responsibilities.

Consider the man from Bethesda. From what we know about him, he didn't have to journey to work each day to earn his living, he didn't have to support a family, and, in general, much less was expected from him than from a normal, healthy male of his day. In fact, people catered to him. They carried him to the pool and chances are the welfare system of that day fed and clothed him and met his basic needs. In short, people expected very little from the Bethesda man and consequently, upon examination, the question, Do you want to be healed? was a legitimate one.

Many of us must answer that same question today for we've learned that our ailments reduce the expectations which others and we ourselves have for us and we've become conditioned and comfortable with our minimal output. We are keenly aware that when we're whole, healthy and have it all together, the Lord and others expect more from us. So we hang on to our spiritual ailments.

All of us are ailing in some area of our lives.

Some need to be healed in their attitude towards employment. It's difficult for many of us to have a positive attitude towards work, day in and day out, but God expects us to do *all* unto His glory and that *all* includes our work. When we answer, "Yes, I want to be healed" regarding my employment attitude, our colleagues, employer, and we ourselves have a right to expect increased production.

Some need to be healed in the area of finances. We've

been so pleasure-oriented we've over-extended ourselves, worked our credit cards to their maximum, and for all intents should consider engaging a financial counselor or filing chapter 13 of bankruptcy. To be healed in the financial area will require that we say no to many pleasurable activities, do without additional material things, and render to God that portion of our earnings He deems fair. When healing affects our pocketbook, the "Yes I want to be healed" may not be quick in coming.

Sick Self-Concept

Some need to have our self-concepts healed, for our feelings of inadequacy have made it nearly impossible to live effectively. Those in this category often thrive on being viewed as martyrs, receiving the pity of others. Being healed would eliminate this much sought-after attention.

Helen, by appearance and action, is a stable saint. When the church or a member of the Body has any need, Helen is always there. When evangelistic teams or touring singing groups need a place to stay and a meal, Helen's hand is the first outstretched. When someone is taken ill, Helen almost beats them to the hospital.

Upon close observation, however, one becomes aware that Helen does nothing without making a spiritual martyrdom statement: "I'm just so tired, I could hardly drag myself down here"; "Well, if I didn't have them over for dinner, no one would"; "I've been feeling so bad lately I wouldn't be surprised if they kept me here in the hospital with you," and so it goes.

Helen has a self-concept problem. While her deeds are worthy, she is obviously parading her good deeds from a motivation to be seen as an oppressed martyr for the cause of Christ. Unfortunately, if we read her correctly, Helen's only reward will be here on earth, for Jesus told us, "Beware of practicing your righteousness before men to be noticed by them; otherwise you have no reward with your Father who is in heaven'' (Matt. 6:1).

Helen's spiritual hypochondria is preventing her from effective, joyful service. Being healed would result in continued good service, but her motivation would be solely her desire to glorify God, without drawing attention to herself.

Emotional Hypochondria

Some need to be healed emotionally for, although they evidence a sound body and mind, their emotional instability renders them ineffective. But they refuse to relinquish emotional crutches and seek healing for fear that more will be expected of them or that they may fail to achieve their desired goals.

Tom had achieved assistant manager status of a large store before his thirtieth birthday, only one step away from his goal of store manager. To assure him the greatest chance of promotion, he completed two additional years of management training; yet time and time again he was overlooked while others received his coveted prize.

Each time Tom was passed over he blamed his failure on his former manager who had not given him a wholehearted supportive recommendation. Recently Tom questioned the administrator in charge of promotions; this man indicated Tom's failure to be elevated to store manager was due to his inability to make critical decisions.

Tom cannot accept this explanation and is now seeking new employment because he knows he's been blackballed.

When I asked Tom, why he didn't take a seminar in decision-making to attempt to bolster his skills, he indicated, ''It's no use.''

Many of us, like Tom, need to be healed emotionally so we can accept and evaluate the facts as they are before taking appropriate action; but if we did, would that allow us to explain our lack of success? By claiming that we are not treated fairly we never have to accept a valid criticism.

Ailing Relationships

While many other areas of our life may require healing, probably none is more critical or requires a greater effort or time commitment than the area of relationships.

When Jesus asks me, "Do you want to be healed in the area of relationships?" I first must define which relationship, then must determine whether I'm willing to commit the time and effort necessary to aid the healing process with the full knowledge that healing will mandate increased expectations.

Sometimes the relationship needing the most attention is my relationship with the Lord, at other times my relationship with my wife or children must top the priority list.

Examine your present relationship needs and before answering "Yes, I want to be healed," or "No, I don't want to be healed," determine which relationship needs the greatest improvement and then answer accordingly.

Jerry's marriage was in serious trouble for he and Marge had not been communicating well for the last several years. He had resolved to talk to Marge about their relationship on several occasions yet each time failed to discuss it.

Finally one night he blurted out, "Marge, I think we need counseling." At first Marge throught he was kidding, but soon sensed his seriousness and suggested they talk. She refused to seek counseling until, "We spend some time together trying to solve our own problem."

Jerry was crushed and inwardly felt that her refusal to seek a counselor reflected her feelings that their relationship was not that important. He also resented the fact that she seemed to indicate that the problem, if any, was his, not hers.

Rocky months followed that first discussion and one morning Jerry abruptly left home. Marge was crushed and couldn't conceal the heartbreak she felt, despite her efforts to mask her feelings. She felt as if her world had crumbled.

Jerry visited his close friend in the weeks which followed. Although his friend encouraged Jerry to adhere to his marital commitment, seek counseling and make a total effort towards healing the relationship, Jerry expressed grave concerns.

"I don't know if I really love her anymore. I've got to determine that before we decide on seeing a counselor. Besides, if we got our relationship squared away, I really doubt that I could contribute what I should to making my marriage a good one. I'm actually afraid of the prospect of failure."

How sad, but far too frequently true. Many of us, like Jerry, fear the total healing of a relationship for fear we'll not be able to comply with our new requirements and expectations.

We may refuse His offer to heal our relationships for many reasons.

The absence of love. When one seriously questions whether love exists in the relationship they frequently are unwilling to expend the effort required in the healing process.

Pride. It's difficult for many of us and nearly impossible for others to admit we have a problem, for this admission shows everyone that we're not self-sufficient. We also feel that openly acknowledging our problem lowers our position in the eyes of others.

Vulnerability. All of us hate to admit we're vulnerable yet failure to do so precludes our being helped.

Increased expectations. Anyone involved in a relationship in the process of being healed automatically seems to expect more from the healed party.

Fear. These increased expectations cause fear of failure to mount. "Can I live up to what's expected of me?" becomes a vital concern.

Fear of intimacy. Healing in a relationship assumes increased intimacy. Some, uncomfortable with surface relationships, become terrorized when they consider increased intimacy.

Do You Want to Be Healed?

Grandma Bates openly complained from the moment I met her. She never offered a positive response to the question, "How are you?" Even when she looked excellent she uttered, "Well, not so bad, my throat hurts and the doctor says nothing's wrong."

Indeed he had, and so had five other doctors. When their tests proved negative and they offered, "There's nothing wrong with you," she'd trot off to another doctor until she found one who'd agree to prescribe medicine.

She seemed to delight in people talking of her plight and offering condolences at her condition.

When her son elicited all the reasons she had for being thankful and happy she offered a barrage of reasons to assure him that her present problems far overshadowed her blessings. Soon her son adjusted to the situation. He finally recognized that she did not want to be healed for fear she'd lose the attention of others.

While some, for a variety of reasons, answer "No, I don't want to be healed," others submit to the healing process and quickly discover that the joy they find through healing is so great, it overshadows any and all accompanying liabilities.

Before answering yes to our Lord's question, "Do you want to be healed?" we must first be willing to ask ourselves these questions:

"Do I really want to be healed?" Until we come to the point where we can resoundingly answer yes, the healing process will be inept.

"Am I willing to pay the price?" The healing process, while sometimes instantaneous, often requires a long trip through deep emotional hurt and offensive memories. The person who begins the healing process with a halfhearted commitment to endure whatever comes with it, will frequently abandon ship.

"Will I use all available resources to effect a cure?" Do I

have any hang-ups about seeking the Lord, using professional counselors, or committing my needs and hurts to my God in prayer? If I do, the healing process could be a long and arduous process *if* it occurs.

The Lord uses a variety of resources in the healing process and our openness to all of them facilitates His work.

Yes, Lord, I want to be healed.

Please make me sensitive to the areas where my life is hurting and incomplete.

Create within me such an intense desire to be healed that I'll be willing to submit to whatever is necessary to make wholeness a reality.

In anticipation of the great joy I know will result, I thank you.

Exercise for Understanding

Do you agree or disagree with the following statements?

	agree	disagree
1. When I admit my vulnerability or need for help, it sometimes gives confidence and assurance to others.	☐	☐
2. Healing is as important a part of ministry as Bible teaching.	☐	☐
3. Most healing takes place in a spectacular manner (i.e. TV crusade).	☐	☐
4. If we are honest, we all have need of healing.	☐	☐
5. If my faith is strong enough, I should discontinue being treated by professionals and rely totally on the Lord for healing.	☐	☐

	agree	disagree
6. It is more difficult for men to seek healing than it is for women.	☐	☐
7. People who have experienced a healing feel more obligated to assist others whom they see suffering.	☐	☐

16
Overcoming the Blahs

At the outset of this book I asked, "Is it possible to live consistently on a spiritual high?" We've discussed some of the reasons for the blahs and what we can do to lessen their frequency while steadily growing towards Christian joy.

Growth towards Christian joy and abundant life offered by Jesus Christ is an ongoing process which begins when we invite Jesus into our life and reaches perfection on that glorious day when He bursts through the clouds to take us to Himself.

Most of us are presently spinning our wheels in neutral somewhere between the beginning (our salvation experience) and our eternal reward (heaven). The lack of progress we're experiencing provides ample rationale for the frustrations and blahs present in our daily lives.

I've shared with you some of the traps to which I've fallen prey. They have prevented me from experiencing the joy and fulfillment which is rightfully mine as a child of the King. Undoubtedly, you too, could share the pitfalls you've encountered in your search for the abundant life.

Evaluate Your Life

Examination of our lives in this questioning manner is an absolute necessity if we are to attain the joy God promised.

Jesus Christ expects us to question our established life patterns, for without an ongoing evaluation based upon His Word and revelations of His Holy Spirit, stagnancy is inevitable.

To close our minds to potential change and growth demonstrates we're satisfied with stagnancy. If we use our God-given common sense and rely on the Holy Spirit to reveal and clarify the mind-set and behavior patterns which are robbing us of joy, the time and frequency we spend in the pits will be greatly lessened.

Relying on the Holy Spirit entails providing the vehicles (i.e. Bible reading, prayer, and fellowship) through which He speaks to us.

Proceed to Correct the Problem

Once we've examined our lives and gained new insights our lives will still be deficient in joy until we act upon our new findings by altering or eliminating our destructive thoughts or behavior.

Just as Jesus said, "Therefore everyone who hears these words of Mine, and *acts upon them,* may be compared to a wise man" (Matt. 7:24), so discovering truths in our lives only becomes profitable and wise when we combine our discovery with action.

In fact, let's go one step further. Once we discover truth about ourselves and fail to take corrective action, our level of frustration and guilt increases and our self-concept decreases as we continue wallowing in our stagnancy and miserableness.

Even the apostle Paul, whose life seemed to be above reproach, was motivated to continue towards Christian maturity and the joyful, abundant life when he wrote, "Not that I have already obtained it, or have already become perfect, but I press on in order that I may lay hold of that for which also I was laid hold of by Christ Jesus. . . . But one thing I do: forgetting what lies behind and reaching forward to what lies ahead, I press on toward the goal for the prize of the upward call of God in Christ Jesus'' (Phil. 3:12-14).

Reach Forward to Better Things

Paul reinforced our need to examine our life by Christ's standards but then added the all important second dimension when he encouraged us to forget about our past, including those behavior patterns which have kept us from the abundant life, while *reaching forward* to the better things which lie ahead.

When we've examined our life to determine the reasons for our blahs and discouragements, and feel the Holy Spirit has shown what is robbing us of joy, we are to put the detrimental behavior behind us and implement more constructive behavior.

By our nature, we are creatures of habit. Unless we have divine assistance, we'll often regress to our pre-established behavior patterns. Yet despite Christ's offer, how many of us have ever really prayed for joy, fulfillment, and the abundant life?

I've prayed for provisions, jobs, people, forgiveness, salvation, material possessions, safety, children, wisdom and a myriad of other things but never, ever prayed for joy. Yet Scripture tells us, ''You do not have because you do not ask'' (Jas. 4:2).

After discovering what may be stealing our joy, we must put it behind us, attempt to consciously implement the new strategy, ask our Saviour for the joy He told us could be ours, and thank Him in advance for the joy and abundance we know we'll receive.

My life is by no means an example of pure joy; yet, when I apply this formula to a problem area in my life, new joy and fulfillment become immediately evident.

It often takes a good case of the blahs to cause us to

recognize our depraved condition and instill within us a desire to seek a more joyous life. The words of a contemporary Christian song convey the thought well:

Down isn't so bad
When it gets you lookin' up at life
To see where you've been now
And don't wanna be there again.

You already knew
That you were getting through to me
It must have been so tough
To get me lookin' up.

Well, there are times we all fall in
Much too deep where we can't swim.
But there's a lifesaver
To keep us from cashin' it in.

Well, down is where you found me
But up is where I'm goin'.
Now that you're around me
I can't keep it from showin';
Grinnin' on my face
And singin' every place I go.

Well, down is where you found me
But up is where I'm goin'.
Finally understand
All the things I've been knowin'.
Take me in your arms
And carry me all the way home. [1]

Our downs, at times, serve to point us towards the Saviour and interaction with Him gives us, like the disciples, great joy (see Luke 24:52).

We're guilty of negligence when we become aware that our lives could be more joyous and abundant yet fail to act in concert with God's Word to move closer to collecting on His promises. He alone has the power to raise us from the *pits* to the *peaks* yet because He chose to give us our own free will, He needs our willing cooperation to make true joy a reality.

Lord, I praise you for the difficult circumstances I've experienced getting to this point in my life, and for the pressures I feel in my present situation. I never have totally understood your reasons for allowing my downs, my heartaches, my anxieties and my inner turmoil, yet I accept them knowing they are part of your plan to make me into the total person you desire me to be.

Deep down I'd be disappointed if I could comprehend your purposes, for then my intelligence would question your suitability to be worshiped.

Thanks for all the things you've pointed out to me. Keep them fresh on my mind and sensitize me through your Holy Spirit to recognize even more, so that I may spend a minimal amount of time with the blahs and a maximum amount of time experiencing your joy.

Note

1. "Down Isn't So Bad," © 1977 by Home Sweet Home Music. Print rights administered by Word Music, Inc. Used by permission.